Mama Nazima's
Jewish-Iraqi
Cuisine

Mama Nazima's Jewish-Iraqi Cuisine

Cuisine, history, cultural references, and survival stories of the Jewish-Iraqi

Rivka Goldman

HIPPOCRENE BOOKS
NEW YORK

This book is a journey through Jewish life in Iraq.

Ancient prayer for protection: May this prayer shine on you each time you use this book.

Paperback edition, 2021
Copyright © 2006 by Rivka Goldman.
All rights reserved.

Cover and book design by Acme Klong Design, Inc.
Front cover photography by Madeline Polss
Photography by Rivka Goldman
All unlabeled photos are from various markets in the United States

For more information, address:

HIPPOCRENE BOOKS, INC.
171 Madison Avenue
New York, NY 10016

ISBN 978-0-7818-1426-3
Previous edition ISBN 978-0-7818-1144-6

This book is dedicated to my mother, Leah Nazima Sofer, who raised seven children and twenty grandchildren and loved them all equally.

Her creativity made a significant mark on her artwork, cooking, and practice of ancient medicine. She was a healer, and nourished the ill and the needy. She assisted many brides who otherwise could not have afforded the expense of wedding dresses by sewing and donating their bridal gowns. My mother enriched her home with magnificent meals and laughter.

She was not only a cook but also a pillar of strength for her family and her community.

When my mother died, hundreds of people wept and mourned her death. At her funeral, buses were rented to accommodate the multitudes who escorted her to her final resting place. My mother touched the hearts of many people and made a difference in their lives. She touched my heart and left me with memories and profound gratitude.

No words can express my thanks to my mother, who inspired me to write this book and share her nutritious recipes.

Acknowledgments

For the Jewish-Iraqi people, hospitality is a creed rather than an obligation. My family members have maintained a tradition of hospitality through generations. This book is a memento of their support and desire to preserve our heritage.

Special thanks are extended to my husband Bob, our son Nir, my brother Eli, and my aunt Habiba for their ideas and support. Many thanks are due my daughters Liat and Liliana, and my brothers Oved and Menashe and their families, for their love of my cooking. They have shared their enthusiasm with their friends, many of whom have eaten at my family's table.

Table of Contents

Introduction

The value of nutrition is an important facet of Jewish-Iraqi cuisine. Although these recipes are based on ancient tradition, their standards are in agreement with current dietetic knowledge. The modern concept is that nutrients provide energy to maintain growth and support life. The ancient view is that food enhances one's strength, as directly expressed in the Jewish Arabic "*El akle yitahe kowa.*" I remember my mother saying "*T'ayno akle hatar yekbar*" which means "Give him food so he can grow."

Whenever I read about the relationship of proper nutrition to the immune system, I hear an echo of my mother's suggestions for those who sought her help. As a healer, she advised others on proper food choices and avoiding foods that might impair their health. The idea that proper nutrition has an impact on our immune system has its roots in ancient medicine. One can strengthen one's immune system through nutrition, lifestyle, and attitude.

In order to maintain a healthy diet, one must consume protein-rich food, such as poultry, fish, or lean meat; also, complex carbohydrates, high fibers, vegetables and fruit. The use of all of these is emphasized in the recipes in this book, which are given in their authentic form, except that they have been modified to provide low-fat, low-cholesterol alternatives to their originals. My mother taught me to make such conversions, and it is my hope that these recipes will in turn increase your desire to stay healthy while enjoying exotic food.

A Brief Jewish-Iraqi History

I was born in an ancient land and grew up surrounded by an ancient culture. Basra, the southern port city of Iraq, is my birthplace. The Tigris and Euphrates rivers run through it, joining to form the Shaat al Arab River that empties into the Persian Gulf.

This area of Iraq (once called Mesopotamia) has been linked with Jewish history since biblical times. According to the Bible, Iraq is supposedly the site of the Garden of Eden (Genesis 2:14) and the birthplace of Abraham, the first Jew, who migrated from the city of Ur of the Chaldees to the current state of Israel (Genesis 11: 27-29). Subsequently, after enslavement by the pharaohs in Egypt and salvation by Moses, Moses and Joshua led the Hebrews to Israel, where they gained independence and religious freedom.

After several hundred years, the first Hebrew kingdom was established under King Saul, who was followed by King David around the year 1000 B.C. His son, King Solomon, built the First Holy Temple in Jerusalem, extending the Hebrew realm to a large area beyond the original borders of the state. During the succeeding period, the Middle East was dominated by the kingdoms of Mesopotamia, Assyria, and Babylonia. After much struggle with the latter two, Jerusalem was destroyed by the Babylonian emperor Nebuchadnezar in 586 B.C., and the Jews were exiled to what is now Iraq.

There has been a Jewish presence in Iraq since that time. Although the Persian emperor Cyrus allowed Jews to return to Jerusalem in 530 B.C., many chose to remain in the area, where they maintained their identity, religion, and culture. Jews in Iraq prayed at the shrine of Ezekiel, the prophet, until the exodus from Iraq in the twentieth century.

For the six hundred years following the restoration of the Holy Temple and the city of Jerusalem, the Jews remaining in Iraq formed an important center of population known as *Golah* ("The Captivity") and maintained a close connection with the Jews in Israel. The destruction of Jerusalem and the Second Temple by the Romans under the emperor Titus in A.D. 70 and the decline of the Roman Empire led to a deterioration of conditions and increasing disorder in all Roman-occupied lands. As a result, many Jews migrated to Mesopotamia, where they were safe and welcome. Over many centuries the large community there developed a post-Biblical Jewish religious and intellectual tradition. The resulting scholarly center had a significant influence on the future of worldwide Jewish life. Its greatest achievement was the development of the Babylonian Talmud, which presents laws for Jewish living, including ritual cleansing, dietary practices, and the observance of holidays.

The Arab conquests of the seventh and eighth centuries did not strongly affect the core of Jewish life. The community was able to retain its prominence as a center of Jewish learning. Although the Jews shared some of their neighbors' traditions, they kept their own identity, education, unique Arabic dialect, and cuisine. However, by the end of the first millennium, there was a sharp decline in the vitality of Jewish life in Iraq, caused by economic factors. Overfarming led to a decrease in soil fertility, and there were increasing opportunities in the developing Western lands such as Spain, which had come under Moslem rule.

By the thirteenth century the Mongol conquests destroyed the Islamic theocracy centered in Iraq. This led to a period of several centuries during which the Jews in Iraq were under Persian rule. In 1534, after a long series of wars between the Iranian shahs and the Ottoman Turks, Iraq was conquered by the Ottomans, who controlled it until the end of World War I.

Toward the end of the Ottoman rule, the Jews were exposed to an active hostility. The decline of Ottoman power led to less tolerance of minorities in general. It was natural that hostility should be directed at the Jews, who had much less access to European protection than did the Christian minorities.

As a result, the Jews no longer felt safe living in the region. Some migrated to India or other neighboring countries. This migration and the opening of the Suez Canal allowed for Jewish involvement in international trade. Once more the Iraqi Jews flourished, and many moved to Basra, the southern port city.

After the final defeat and destruction of the Ottoman Empire in World War I, the victorious allies, Britain and France, gained control of most of the Middle East. Britain secured a League of Nations mandate over Iraq, specifically. The British occupation, which lasted between 1917 and 1932, resulted in the improvement of Jewish education, particularly the establishment of foreign-language training in Jewish schools. This furthered the Jewish role in trade and led to the economic development of the community.

With the advent of Nazism during World War II, persecution of the Jews increased. In May 1941, there was a day of, *El Farhud* (pogrom), during which Arabs and Bedouins, influenced by Nazi propaganda with government approval, killed many Jews, stole their possessions, and destroyed their property. The worsening security conditions led many to fear for their lives. Large numbers, in particular the young, escaped Iraq—braving the dangers of capture.

In 1950, the Iraqi government allowed the Jews to leave, provided that they relinquish their citizenship and all their possessions. There was a massive exodus, and almost all of the Jewish population emigrated to Israel.

Culinary Skills and Culture

Although Jewish Iraqis could not bring their material possessions to Israel, they brought their knowledge and culture—and many recipes from their rich and exotic cuisine.

The Israeli society which they encountered was largely European in background and oriented towards different foods, kitchen equipment, and cooking methods. However, as a whole, Jewish Iraqis preferred their own ways; not only did they keep their original ways of cooking, but they also established a special market in Petach Tikvah, near Tel Aviv. The market is full of stores and restaurants, selling both ingredients and prepared dishes from the entire range of Jewish-Iraqi cuisine. The availability of these resources makes it easy to sustain this culinary heritage and encourages its continuation.

The utensils and the type of heat available often determine the style of cooking as well. In the first few years after the establishment of the state of Israel in 1948, ovens were scarce for the immigrants. We cooked our meals over low heat on small pilot gas burners. My mother's cooking followed this tradition, and I, too, tend to reduce heat in cooking a meal, simmering it over a low flame. I have found that this allows the ingredients to blend, making for delightful aromas and flavors. I have emphasized this low heat technique in this book.

My mother was the original source of my recipes. As a healer, she integrated hygiene and healthful food preparation. Washing hands was an important part of the cooking process. Vegetable or olive oil replaced animal fat in her cooking.

The ritual of serving food characterizes the Jewish-Iraqi way of living. Hospitality is a creed and one of the leading principles of our life. The house is always open to outsiders. Traditionally, the welcoming of the guests is both a pleasure and an honor. They are always served first. It is common when preparing food to make enough for unexpected visitors. This practice is reminiscent of the patriarch Abraham who welcomed the three angels to his tent in the desert and served them food.

The code of etiquette for serving also expresses additional underlying social rules. Before marriage, the bride-to-be sits at a table beside the groom. She is honored by the groom's family as a guest. Once she is married, her role is reversed, and she becomes the one to render service to visitors through her cooking. Within the family, the elderly are respected and served ahead of others, and small children are cared for before the older ones.

Culinary skill is a highly respected accomplishment for the women; very few Jewish Iraqi men cook. We always prepare food to suit the taste of those who will eat it. We need and expect their approval. I find myself following this tradition, always asking how the food tastes. My husband often responds by noting the success of a dish.

Cooking is a soothing activity for Iraqi Jews. It can be creative and enjoyable. Although some of the dishes in this book require lengthy preparation, most of the recipes are short and simple. Some of the dishes, however, can be assembled a day in advance to allow the spices to blend together so that the taste becomes richer.

Jewish-Iraqi cuisine makes ample use of what the earth offers. The diet is rich in vegetables, which are abundant in both Iraq and Israel, and the art of combining spices for taste and aroma plays an important role in the cuisine. Blending the spices and herbs together makes each meal a feast. Such herbs as thyme, sage, basil, and oregano leave a fragrant trail throughout the preparation, cooking, and serving of the meal.

Because of Iraq's location at the crossroads of many trade routes, merchants brought herbs and spices from neighboring countries as well as from the Far East. Therefore we use an enormous range of spices in our cuisine. I remember as a child in Basra, there was a street containing small spice shops. In Israel, in the markets of cities such as Jerusalem, Tel Aviv and Rehovot, shops sell nothing but herbs and spices. Fresh herbs are often used in salads and various other dishes, such as: dill for fish, and mint and parsley for salads. Such spices as ground turmeric and mango powder are used for color and a slightly acidic taste.

My mother adhered to certain practices such as the usage of cardamom, cinnamon, ginger, basil, mint, dill, and lemon to aid with digestion. People who ate her cooking did not feel tired or sluggish, but instead content and desirous of eating more of her tasty foods. Another belief was that honey and ground almonds mixed with sugar should be given to a woman after she had given birth to enhance her endurance, remove sadness, and protect her from the evil eye. Other beliefs are associated with colors. Eating yellow vegetables such as crookneck squash results in laughter and happiness. Green zucchini and green apples are also considered sources of hope and prosperity. The color black is thought to be unlucky; traditionally we peel the eggplant prior to cooking.

Various customs of the neighboring peoples were incorporated into Jewish Iraqi culture as well. Garlic is believed by some to ward off the evil eye, and is hung at the front door of the house to protect its inhabitants from danger. Door posts on new homes are marked with a palm print to protect the home and keep away harm. This ancient Jewish-Iraqi practice is a simulation of the Biblical marking of door posts to avert the Angel of Death during the exodus from Egypt. The custom has become part of the Jewish ritual of *Chanukat Ha-bayit* (the blessing of the new home).

The Idiom of Iraqi Jewish Arabic

Iraqi Jews speak Jewish Arabic, a dialect unique to us. Metaphor-rich expressions with allusions to food, spiritual belief, and personal behavior are used on a daily basis. They are an integral part of our life, used to describe events, circumstances, and relationships, among my favorite sayings being

"*Mani yakle al ein au el'thum*" ("Who desires the food, the eyes or the mouth?")—once you see the food, you desire to eat it. Other examples found throughout this book are:

"*Yom assal, yom basal*" ("a day of honey, a day of onion")—one day brings happiness, and another sadness.

"*Alla ma yinshaf bl'akel yinabad*" ("One cannot see G-d, but in our mind we worship him.") This refers to the idea that if we use our mind to believe in G-d's existence even though we cannot see him, we can also use our intellect to make proper choices on a daily basis.

"*Katalni wah baka, sbakni wah shtaka*" ("He struck me and hastened to cry, then raced to complain")—referring to an aggressive individual who abuses others and pretends that he is the victim.

This book includes recipe names and metaphorical phrases representing the food and culture of the Iraqi Jews, all written in the traditional, oral Jewish Arabic dialect, rather than the classical Arabic.

Holidays, spiritual beliefs, and cuisine

Iraqi Jews developed many special new customs. For each day and for each holiday, new practices arose, which in time became traditions. Each of the cultures that has entered into Israeli society has contributed its own culinary influence, and a diverse cuisine has emerged. However, Iraqi Jews have modified some recipes to fit our own cuisine. For example, *burekas*, brought to Israel by Greek, Bulgarian, and Turkish Jews, have been changed by using spices and vegetables, such as cumin, ginger, nutmeg, basil, green chile peppers, curry, coriander, paprika, spinach, celery, potatoes, tomatoes, and onions.

People always turn to food to mark such important events as holidays, weddings, births, and bar mitzvahs. These occasions are celebrated with a variety of sweet, colorful, and spicy dishes, depending on the season and the availability of fruit and vegetables. In addition, there are a few specific recipes for each holiday which are included in this book.

Saturday is a day of rest. All of our meals are prepared on Friday and cooked over low heat overnight, to be served warm on Saturday. Traditionally, *Shabbat* eggs (eggs cooked in tea, page 58), turnips, and quince are included. The main meal is the *tebit*, chicken stuffed with meat and rice (page 121-122).

Like all Jews, we welcome *Shabbat* with the Friday night meal, which includes the lighting of candles and the blessings of the wine and food. Blessing the bread while it is dipped in salt is part of the *Shabbat* ritual. In the Jewish-Iraqi tradition, salt is a symbol of life and family ties, which have always been enhanced by celebrating and honoring the *Shabbat*.

There is also a specific ritual in honor of the mother for maintaining the household and caring for her husband and children. Her role as a woman, wife, and mother is celebrated through the chanting of the *Ashet Chayil* ("Woman of Valor") psalm with a special, Jewish-Iraqi melody. Over many, many years, this ancient song has been brought from Iraq to Israel and is continued in our homes in the United States.

The Jewish New Year is celebrated with blessings for symbolic foods, including apples, leeks, dates, squash, zucchini, black eyed-peas, pomegranates, collard greens, and the head of a fish. The Jewish-Iraqi names for the above foods interplay with the Hebrew words; for instance in Jewish Arabic "*karh*" means "squash" while in Hebrew it means "a tear or a rip." Blessing the squash symbolizes the wish for the tearing away of, or the removal of, a disastrous event and its replacement with hope and salvation. Blessing a fish head symbolizes the wish to be a leader and not fall behind.

The Sukkoth holiday commemorates the wanderings of the Jews in the desert between the exodus from Egypt and the entrance to Israel. The *Sukkah* hut symbolizes the first stopping place of the Hebrews after leaving Egypt and it must be under the open sky. In Iraq, because the homes were built with the first floor open to the sky, the *Sukkah* could be built inside the walls of the house.

In Israel, the *Sukkah* is built out of doors. It is always decorated with dates, pomegranates, figs, apples, myrtle branches, palms, willows, etrog and other fruits and vegetables. Date cookies (Date cookies page 167) and citrus food dishes (Tomato orange salad page 17) are eaten in the *Sukkah*; during the holiday, all meals are eaten there as well.

Historically, Hanukkah is a holiday of freedom. It celebrates the successful Maccabean revolt against the Hellenistic Syrians, who occupied Jerusalem and the Second Temple in the second century B.C. When the Maccabees recovered the Temple, they found only enough oil to light the menorah for one day. Miraculously the oil lasted for eight days until more could be obtained.

Hanukkah is celebrated with many sweets and potato dishes which are prepared differently by people from different countries. The Iraqi Jews make *kba* dumplings, a potato dough stuffed with chicken, meat, and raisins (see page 107-108). When we moved to Israel, we adopted additional foods and modified them to fit our cuisine. For example, to Eastern European potato pancakes, or latkes, we added Iraqi spices.

The *tu Bishvat* holiday, the "holiday of the trees" marks the beginning of spring. It is customary to plant trees in Israel and to eat dried fruit and nuts at this time. Many dishes such as *tershana* (see page 69) and *luzinah* (see page 177).

Purim is of particular significance to Iraqi Jews, because its events involved Babylonian Jews in exile from the First Temple. The holiday commemorates how the Jewish queen Esther and her uncle Mordecai saved the Jews from destruction at the hands of Haman, advisor to the Persian king. Later it was the Persian king Cyrus who allowed the Jews to return to Jerusalem and rebuild the Temple in 480 B.C.

A variety of such sweets as *zingulah* (see page 174) and *luzinah* (see pages 176) are served during Purim. The eating of these sweets and the recounting of the story of Queen Esther are favorite practices for both children and adults. It is customary for friends and families to exchange trays of sweets to mark the happiness of the holiday. This tradition of the sending of the portions of food.is called *mishloach manot*.

Passover, the great festival of freedom, celebrates the exodus of the Hebrews under the leadership of Moses from the bondage of the pharaohs of Egypt.

Most Jewish holidays are celebrations of freedom and hope. During Passover, Iraqi Jewish adults as well as children, act out the story of the exodus from Egypt. All children carry bags on their backs, and some portray elderly people by walking with canes. The adults ask the questions: "Who are you?" "Where are you coming from?" and "Where are you going?" Children sing the answers: "We are the Hebrews from Egypt and we are on our way to Jerusalem." This reenactment establishes Jewish identity and makes us a part of our history.

It is customary for Jews not to eat leavened bread during Passover. Iraqi Jews have unique dishes for this holiday. Since we (unlike Eastern European Jews) are allowed to eat rice, many dishes are prepared with it (rice with tomato page 145).

One of the most traditional dishes served at Passover is *haroset* (see page 180), which consists of *silan*, a honey-like syrup extracted from dates and blended with ground walnuts and almonds. Although *silan* is served throughout the year, it is used particularly during Passover. *Kahi*, leavened Iraqi pancakes (see page 160), are eaten for breakfast on the first morning after the end of the holiday. They mark the beginning of ordinary days.

The feast of Shavuot takes place forty-nine days after Passover. Shavuot celebrates Moses' reception of the Ten Commandments on Mount Sinai during subsequent Jewish wanderings in the desert. In the time of the Second Temple, it became a great popular festival when pilgrims came to Jerusalem to offer the first fruits at the Temple. In addition, Shavuot occurs at the beginning of June when flowers are in full bloom. Flowers have great meaning to the Iraqi Jews and are often used in their metaphors. For example "*El rehi mal ward atred el aroh*" means "the smell of the flower nourishes the soul."

Iraqi Jews call Shavuot, *Eid el Ziarah*, the holiday of pilgrimage. Historically Babylonian and later Iraqi Jews substituted a journey to Kiffel, the burial place of the prophet Ezekiel, who was originally from Jerusalem. Many Jews visited the tomb, which was surrounded by a large square that could accommodate many people. There, the pilgrims gave their offerings and their prayers.

As a child, I heard many stories about Kiffel and its mystical ways of helping the Jews: Valuable items that had been lost or stolen were found. Sick people prayed for health and got well. The story was told many times of a mother who took her ailing son to Kiffel, wishing for his recovery. At night, when the child fell asleep, a rabbi entered his dream and gave him the name of a physician who could provide a cure. The next morning, the child awoke and told his dream to his mother. Although the physician was unknown to her, because of her strong belief in the spiritual power at Kiffel she took her son to that physician, and the boy was cured.

The strong Jewish-Iraqi belief in mysticism and spirituality aided their existence in a hostile environment. It intensified hope, prayers, and the confidence for salvation. It found expression on a daily basis in the proverb, *Aind alla amah b'aidi* "It is not far from God's reach" which means "Keep on believing, keep on hoping, never give up: miracles can happen."

This mysticism is based on a combination of the Jewish Kabbalah, a religious book, and the adaptations of local beliefs and practices. Salt, which for Iraqi Jews is of particular importance as it is a symbol of life, is offered to Mother Earth in exchange for protection from the evil eye. The ritual of drinking Turkish coffee and predicting the future by reading the pattern of coffee grounds remaining in the cup is used particularly in times of trouble, sickness, and uncertainty. At weddings, the red dye, henna, is put on the palms of the bride and the finger tips of the groom as a beauty aid and to protect the couple from the evil eye.

Foreign Influences on Jewish-Iraqi Cuisine

Foreign influences on Jewish Iraqi cuisine derive from historical military and commercial contacts. I made the connection of one dish with the Mongol conquest through a striking experience: As a child in Iraq, one of my favorite foods was

kemar, thick cream spread on bread and sprinkled with sugar. I had not had this since our exodus from Iraq. To my astonishment, I found that the nomads of the Gobi Desert in Mongolia prepare the same dish, called *urum*, served in the same way to the guests in their *ger* tents. Similarly, such dishes as *kababs* and Turkish coffee, are easily traceable to the period of Ottoman rule.

Commercial contacts with India during the period of European influence are expressed through such dishes as *kitchri* (see page 147) and the pickled mango seasoning, *ambah* (see page 39). Kitchri can be found in both Turkey and India under the same name; however, we modified the recipe with different spices. *Ambah, though uniquely Jewish-Iraqi in color and tast*, is similar to the Indian version of pickled mango, there called *achar*. I have learned from my daughter Liliana that the word *ambah* may have been derived from the Hindi word *aam*, in which means "mango". Similarly, the words *plow* in Jewish Arabic and *pilau* in Hindi both refer to rice pilaf; however, again its recipes are entirely different.

Like the British, we serve afternoon tea with milk, but it is accompanied by fresh bread, feta cheese, Jewish-Iraqi cookies and other desserts (see desserts and jams pages 165-188).

Salads

סלטים

زلأطة

Zlata

Iraqi-Jews serve salad every day.

Salads make ample use of locally grown

fruits and vegetables, and incorporate them

into traditional recipes.

Orange and Tomato Salad

زلأطة طمأطأ وُبرتقالى
Zlata Tamata oo Portkal

The Iraqi Jews developed many customs. For each day and for each holiday, new ideas arose, and in time these ideas became traditions. This salad was created by my mother, who served it to mark the beginning of a sweet year. It became a tradition in our home to have it every New Year.

4 large tomatoes, chopped	¼ cup chopped fresh parsley
4 large oranges, peeled and sliced	¼ cup chopped fresh mint
½ cup (about 6 small) sliced button	⅓ cup raisins
mushrooms	¼ cup sliced almonds

Combine the tomatoes, oranges, mushrooms, parsley, mint, raisins, and almond in a bowl. Chill for ½ hour and serve.

A New Year's Celebration

Once my father told my siblings and I that long, long ago, the Iraqi Jews arranged fruits and vegetables on a New Year's plate in the shape of a tree to symbolize the Tree of Life. The first chapter of Psalms begins with the words "*Etz Haim*" ("Tree of Life"). Each new year, we begin to reread the Torah, which starts with the creation of heaven and earth. The Torah is like a tree which nourishes the soul.

Feta Cheese and Onion Salad

زلأطة بصلى ؤجبن
Zlata Bassal oo Jibin

This warm salad is often served with freshly baked bread, especially on cold winter days.

5 large onions, thinly sliced	*1 pound feta cheese, thickly sliced*

In a pan bring 1 cup of water to a boil. Reduce heat to low and add the onions, cook for 5 minutes, and remove from heat. Stir in the feta cheese, cover, and set aside for 5 minutes. Serve hot.

Mixed Salad

زلاطة مخلؤطة
Zlata Muchluta

The multicolored ingredients in this salad follow the Jewish-Iraqi idea that the visual appearance of food contributes to one's desire to eat it.

4 large tomatoes, diced	**DRESSING:**
½ cup (about 4) chopped scallions	½ teaspoon black pepper
3 large cucumbers, peeled and diced	½ teaspoon ground ginger
1 green bell pepper, cut into small pieces	½ teaspoon garlic powder
½ cup chopped fresh parsley	Juice of 1 large lemon
¼ cup chopped fresh basil	2 teaspoons olive oil
	½ teaspoon salt

Combine the tomatoes, scallions, cucumbers, bell pepper, parsley, and basil in a bowl.

In a second bowl, combine the black pepper, ginger, garlic powder, lemon juice, and olive oil, and pour over the vegetables. Chill for ½ hour. Add the salt just before serving.

Cucumber and Garlic Salad

زلأطة خيأر وُثوُم

Zlata Chyar oo Thum

This is a simple, quickly assembled salad. It suits busy individuals who wish to prepare a fast meal. My mother served it with feta cheese and bread.

8 large cucumbers, peeled and sliced	*3 teaspoons olive oil*
10 cloves garlic, sliced	*½ teaspoon black pepper*
½ cup chopped fresh parsley	*½ teaspoon paprika*
½ cup chopped fresh mint	*½ teaspoon dried dill*
Juice of 4 large lemons	*¾ teaspoon salt*

Combine the cucumbers, garlic, parsley, mint, lemon juice, olive oil, black pepper, paprika, and dill in a bowl, mix, and chill for ½ hour. Add the salt just before serving.

Cucumber and Kohlrabi Salad

زلاطة خيأر وكؤلأرأبى

Zlata Chyar oo Kohlrabi

This salad can be made ahead of time and refrigerated. It is served cold with bread as a snack, or with a main dish, such as chicken.

6 large cucumbers, peeled and sliced	¾ cup white wine vinegar
4 kohlrabi, peeled and sliced	1 teaspoon salt
½ cup chopped fresh parsley	1 teaspoon sugar
5 cloves garlic, sliced	½ teaspoon black pepper
5 fresh bay leaves	

Combine and mix the cucumbers, kohlrabi, parsley, garlic, bay leaves, wine vinegar, salt, sugar, and black pepper in a bowl. Transfer the cucumber mixture to a glass container, and refrigerate for 2 hours. Serve cold.

Cooked Turnips

شلغم مسلؤق
Shalram Musluk

8 SERVINGS

There are many turnip recipes including: boiled turnips, pickled turnips, and turnips stuffed with meat and rice. For this recipe, the turnips were cooked overnight in the oven at a low temperature and traditionally served hot on Saturday morning, to follow the custom that there is no cooking on *Shabbat*. Adapted to a quicker stovetop method, this warm dish is especially welcome during the cool winter.

10 turnips, cleaned, trimmed, and quartered	2 black tea bags
	2 tablespoons sugar

Put the turnips, tea bags, sugar, and 5 cups of water in a pan. Bring to a boil, reduce heat to medium, and cook until the turnips are tender (about 20 minutes). Serve hot or cold.

22

Mama Nazima's Jewish-Iraqi Cuisine

Scallion Salad

8 SERVINGS

بصل ؤذؤمى حأمض
Bassal oo Numi Hamuth

This salad can either accompany a main dish, especially fish, or be served with a sandwich of cold cuts.

3 large lemons	*½ teaspoon black pepper*
3 cups (about 24) chopped scallions	*¼ teaspoon ground nutmeg*
½ teaspoon salt	*¼ teaspoon garlic powder*

Peel the lemons. Remove the pith and seeds. Chop the flesh, and combine it in a bowl with the scallions, salt, black pepper, nutmeg, and garlic. Chill for ½ hour and serve cold.

Cooked Beets

شؤندر مسلؤق
Shwandar Musluk

Beets are commonly boiled, sliced, and dressed with olive oil and lemon juice, sprinkled with parsley and scallions.

8 beets, peeled and diced	*½ teaspoon garlic powder*
2 teaspoons olive oil	*Juice of 1 large lemon*
1 small onion, chopped	*¼ cup chopped fresh parsley*
½ teaspoon salt	*½ cup chopped (about 4) scallions*
½ teaspoon black pepper	

Put the beets in a pot with 3 cups of water and bring to a boil. Reduce heat to medium, cover and cook until tender (about 15 minutes). Drain the water and chill the beets for ½ hour. Heat the olive oil in a skillet and add the onion. Reduce heat to low. Add the salt, black pepper, and garlic, and stir. Cook for additional minute, then remove from heat. Add the lemon juice, parsley, and scallions. Stir the onion mixture into the beets. Serve hot or cold.

Mama Nazima's Jewish-Iraqi Cuisine

Garden Salad

زلأطة مشكلة

Zlata M'shaklah

Any vegetables can go into this salad. The salt is added just before serving to avoid drawing water out of the vegetables.

2 large tomatoes, chopped	**DRESSING:**
½ cup (about 4) chopped scallion	Juice of 1 large lemon
1 large cucumber, peeled and chopped	½ teaspoon black pepper
1 head romaine lettuce, chopped	½ teaspoon garlic powder
½ cup chopped fresh parsley	½ teaspoon ground ginger
1 bell pepper, chopped	½ teaspoon dried oregano
1 cup chopped radishes	½ teaspoon paprika
¼ cup chopped fresh mint	2 teaspoons olive oil
	½ teaspoon salt

Combine the tomatoes, scallions, cucumber, lettuce, parsley, bell pepper, radishes, and mint in a large bowl.

In a second small bowl combine the lemon juice, black pepper, garlic powder, ginger, oregano, and paprika. Add the olive oil and stir to make the salad dressing. Pour it over salad and mix. Add the salt just before serving.

"Sote zangin wala fakir" "Let people label you rich and not poor" describes an individual who to maintain his dignity, does not advertise his financial difficulty. Even if hosts are poor, they provide their guests with many dishes of fruit and vegetables.

Eggplant and Garlic Salad

بأبنجأن مقلى وَّثؤم

Babinjan Mukli oo Thum

This salad is very popular and can be kept in the refrigerator for a week. A pita bread stuffed with a hard-boiled egg topped with Eggplant Garlic Salad makes for a delicious sandwich.

1 large eggplant	5 cloves garlic, sliced
1 teaspoon salt	½ teaspoon white pepper
2 tablespoons vegetable oil	½ teaspoon black pepper
½ cup (about 4) chopped scallions	½ cup cider vinegar
½ cup chopped fresh parsley	

Peel the eggplant and slice ¼ inch thick. Sprinkle the salt over the eggplant, and set aside in a strainer for 1 hour. Squeeze the eggplant slices gently to remove the liquid. Heat the oil and fry the eggplant until browned on both sides. Transfer to a paper towel to drain the oil. Combine the eggplant, scallions, parsley, garlic, white pepper, and black pepper in a bowl and stir in the vinegar. Transfer the eggplant mixture to a glass jar. Chill for 1 hour and serve cold.

Cabbage Salad

زلأطة أبلهذة

Zlata ab L'hana

Prepare this salad a day or two ahead of time, so that the flavor can mellow. Use it as a side dish accompanying a meat meal.

1 head green cabbage, rinsed and chopped	1 teaspoon dried oregano
1 teaspoon salt	½ teaspoon dried sage
½ cup cider vinegar	½ teaspoon garlic powder
	½ teaspoon black pepper

Combine the cabbage and salt in a bowl and set aside for 2 hours to drain the water from the cabbage. Put the cabbage in a pot with 1 cup of fresh water and bring to a boil. Reduce heat to low and simmer until tender (about 15 minutes), then remove the cabbage from heat and cool. Stir in the vinegar, oregano, sage, garlic powder, and black pepper, transfer to a large lidded container and refrigerate (about ½ hour).

Carrot Salad

زلاّطة أبجزغ
Zlata ab Gizar

This delicious carrot salad can be served as an appetizer or during the meal, as a vegetarian side dish on a bed of rice.

1 medium-size onion, chopped	*½ teaspoon red pepper flakes*
1 tablespoon olive oil	*1 teaspoon curry powder*
1½ pounds carrots, peeled and chopped	*Juice of 1 large lemon*
2 stalks celery chopped	*½ teaspoon turmeric*
1 (4-ounce) can tomato sauce	*2 large tomatoes, chopped*
½ teaspoon salt	*1 cup (about 12 small) chopped button*
½ teaspoon garlic powder	*mushrooms*
½ teaspoon black pepper	

Heat the olive oil in a skillet and add the onion. Stir in the carrots and celery over a high heat for 2 minutes. Reduce heat to medium, add 2 cups of water, the

tomato sauce, salt, garlic powder, black pepper, red pepper, curry, lemon juice, and turmeric. Bring to a boil and reduce heat to low. Cover and simmer until tender (about 15 minutes). Add the tomatoes and mushrooms and cook for an additional 2 minutes. Chill, refrigerate, and serve cold.

Potato and Egg Salad

زلأطة بطأطأ وُتحأريج

Zlata Pateta oo Teharige

This potato and egg salad has a definite spicy, slightly acidic taste. Add the salad dressing one hour before serving, to allow the eggs and potatoes to soak up the flavors.

4 large potatoes	**DRESSING:**
2 eggs	*½ cup chopped fresh parsley*
	Juice of 1 large lemon
	½ teaspoon salt
	½ teaspoon black pepper
	½ teaspoon curry powder
	1 tablespoon olive oil

Put the potatoes (unpeeled), eggs, and 3 cups of water in a pot, and boil until the potatoes are tender (about ½ hour). Drain and cool the potatoes and eggs, then peel both. Chop the potatoes and eggs and placed in a salad bowl.

DRESSING:

Combine the parsley, lemon juice, salt, black pepper, curry, and olive oil in a small bowl. Pour the dressing over the salad and mix. Refrigerate for 1 hour and serve cold.

Green Vegetable Salad

زلاطة خضراً
Zlata Chuthra

This salad is extremely simple to make, tastes great, and is easy to digest. Serve it as part of a light meal with feta cheese, olives, and fresh bread. To keep the vegetables crisp, salt the salad immediately before serving to prevent the draining of liquid from the vegetables.

1 head (1 pound) chopped romaine lettuce	**DRESSING:**
1 head (1 pound) chopped chinese cabbage	*Juice of 2 large lemons*
1 cup chopped fresh parsley	*¼ teaspoon ground cardamom*
½ cup chopped fresh basil	*¼ teaspoon ground cinnamon*
1 cup of chopped fresh mint	*½ teaspoon ground ginger*
	½ teaspoon black pepper
	½ teaspoon ground cloves
	1 tablespoon olive oil

In a large bowl combine lettuce, cabbage, parsley, basil, and mint.

DRESSING:
In a second bowl, combine lemon juice, cardamom, cinnamon, ginger, black pepper, and cloves. Stir in the olive oil.

Pour the dressing over the salad, mix, chill, and serve cold.

Cooked Tomato Salad

Bags of the roasted green chile peppers used in this recipe can usually be found in grocery stores. Alternately, you can use 1 (4-ounce) can diced New Mexican green chile peppers.

2 teaspoons vegetable oil	*¼ teaspoon dried thyme*
1 medium-size onion, chopped	*¼ teaspoon dried rosemary*
1 (8-ounce) can tomato sauce	*½ teaspoon dried oregano*
½ cup chopped fresh cilantro	*½ teaspoon black pepper*
3 roasted green chile peppers, chopped	
½ teaspoon curry powder	
Juice of 1 large lemon	*4 large tomatoes, chopped*
½ teaspoon ground ginger	*1 cup (about 8) chopped scallions*
½ teaspoon paprika	

Heat the vegetable oil in a skillet and add the onion. Reduce heat to low, and add 1 cup of water, tomato sauce, cilantro, green chile peppers, curry, lemon juice, ginger, paprika, thyme, rosemary, oregano, and black pepper. Stir and simmer for 10 minutes. Add the tomatoes and simmer for an additional 5 minutes. Remove from heat and add the scallions. Then mix and chill.

Spinach and Leek Salad

زلأطة خضرأ وَكرأث
Zlata ab Chuthra oo K'raf

Spinach and leek salad is well-suited to the busy individual, because it is quick and easy to make. The ingredients should be as fresh as possible.

½ pound leeks	**DRESSING:**
1 pound fresh spinach, stemmed and chopped	Juice of 1 large lemon
	½ teaspoon black pepper
8 ounces feta cheese, cut into small cubes	½ teaspoon ground ginger
4 garlic cloves, sliced	¼ teaspoon ground nutmeg
½ cup (about 4) chopped scallion	½ teaspoon dried oregano
¼ cup chopped fresh basil	2 teaspoons olive oil
4 ounces pitted black olives	

Stem the leeks, separate each leaf, wash under running water to remove all soil, and dry with paper towels. Chop the leeks and combine them with spinach, feta cheese, garlic, scallions, basil, and olives in a bowl.

DRESSING:

In a second bowl combine lemon juice, black pepper, ginger, nutmeg, and oregano. Stir in the olive oil. Pour the dressing over the salad, chill.

Eggplant-Tomato Salad

بأبنجان وطماطا

Babinjan oo Tamata

Eggplant is one of the major ingredients of Jewish-Iraqi cuisine. In Israel, eggplants and tomatoes are available almost always, and this dish is served throughout the year.

---

2 teaspoons olive oil
1 medium-size onion, chopped
1 large eggplant, peeled and chopped
1 (4-ounce) can tomato sauce
¼ cup chopped fresh parsley
¼ cup chopped fresh mint
2 large tomatoes, chopped
3 garlic cloves, crushed

Juice of 1 large lemon
½ teaspoon salt
½ teaspoon ground ginger
½ teaspoon curry powder
½ teaspoon white pepper
½ teaspoon paprika
¼ teaspoon red pepper flakes

Heat the olive oil in a skillet and add the onion. Stir in the eggplant over a high heat. Reduce heat to medium. Add 1 cup of water, tomato sauce, parsley, and mint. Cook until the eggplant is semi-tender (about 10 minutes).

Reduce heat to low and add tomatoes, garlic, lemon juice, salt, ginger, curry, white pepper, paprika, and red pepper, then stir. Cover and simmer till eggplant becomes tender (about 10 minutes). Serve hot or cold.

Escape

A day of mourning and fasting was declared to honor the memory of Shafiq Adas, who had been a very wealthy Jewish merchant. He was well-known to both the Jewish and Arab communities, and had connections with the highest-ranking Iraqi officials. We were told an Iraqi sheikh had told him that he would be accused of being a Zionist and of smuggling arms to Israel unless Adas paid the shiekh a large sum of money. Adas refused to surrender to the extortion, thinking that his wealth and connections to the government guaranteed his safety. On the contrary, he was falsely charged, arrested, and hanged in public. None of his influential government friends came to his rescue. An example was made of him for all the Jews to see: that those who would seek or support Zionism, would meet a fate similar to that of Adas. Indeed Iraqi Jews had learned a lesson: to submit to bribery in order to survive.

So it was with my father. He gave bribes, and was known to the Iraqis as a generous and hospitable man. Nevertheless, one evening, one of his non-Jewish friends informed him that my three eldest brothers were on a police list of Zionists to be captured and imprisoned. That night, my father arranged to have my brothers smuggled out of Iraq through an underground Jewish organization. I remember that they were dressed in many layers of clothing, valuables and cash hidden in various pockets. I recall that I was hushed by my mother for crying out and trying to hang on to them so that they could not go. "The neighbors might hear," she said. I sat quietly, hugging my knees, and did not make any other sound.

Many other Jewish families had done the same. The children collected by the organization and then divided into smaller groups for greater safety in crossing the border to Iran. As a result, my brothers were separated. The youngest one was only eight years old. By that time, it had become known to the Iraqi officials that many Jews were illegally emigrating from Basra to Israel via Iran, with assistance from bribable Iraqis. Various army troops were sent to track, capture, and imprison the illegal emigrants. Although some were captured, many escaped. In spite of the horror of being captured, many more continued to leave Iraq.

My eldest brother's group was spotted by Iraqi troops, so its leader changed the route. They walked through the desert for three days while the troops continued their search by tracking their footsteps. At the end of the third day, when they thought that they had escaped the troops, they reached the Shaat Al Arab where the Tigris and Euphrates rivers join. They were to be transported in pairs across the water to Iran, but the soldiers were waiting for them. Instantly, my brother's group leader took a shawl from one member, spread it out, and requested that all the members of the group empty their pockets onto it. They made a pile of money, jewels, and gold. The leader offered the treasure to the commander of the troops in exchange for letting them cross the border. The money, the jewels, and the gold was too great a temptation to the soldiers, a temptation that saved the lives of my brother and the others.

My three brothers were reunited in Israel. Although each lived in a different kibbutz, they were able to visit one another.

I had always wondered how anyone could send an eight-year-old child alone, across the desert, to another country. I finally understood when I worked with the Bedouins in the Sinai Peninsula. An eight-year-old boy is considered to be a man, and is no longer the responsibility of his mother. My parents sent their eight-year-old to give him a chance to survive despite the unknown outcome of his journey.

Pickles

חמוצים

طرشى

Turshee

Traditionally, all meals are accompanied by a
variety of pickles made from fruit and vegetables.
This book includes recipes for the following
kinds of pickles: mango, turnip,
mixed vegetable, cucumber, and lemon.
All pickles should be kept in sanitized jars.

Pickled Mango

عمبة

Ambah

Pickled mango (*ambah*) is served with most meals, especially for Saturday brunch. It is spread on pita bread and topped with eggs and mixed salad. *Ambah* is also served in meat, chicken, and fish sandwiches.

¼ cup salt	1 tablespoon ground ginger
1 tablespoon turmeric	1 teaspoon black pepper
1 tablespoon curry powder	4 large unpeeled mangoes, diced
2 tablespoons lemon crystal (see below)	

One of the ingredients of all Jewish-Iraqi pickles is lemon crystal, which can be found in any Middle Eastern grocery store. It is powdered lemon juice, bulked up by citric acid. It dissolves readily, tastes like lemon, and is frequently used in Jewish-Iraqi cuisine.

Sanitize the jars (see below).

Combine the salt, turmeric, curry, lemon crystal, ginger, and black pepper in a large bowl with 3 cups of water. Set aside for 15 minutes. Add the mangoes to spice mixture.

Transfer the mixture to sanitized jars (see side bar). Seal and keep at room temperature for 3 days to allow the mangoes to pickle, then refrigerate. *Ambah* ages well and can stay for a year.

The Sanitization of Glass Jars

Clean the jars with soap and hot water, and rinse well. In a large pot bring water to a boil over high heat. Reduce heat to low and add the jars so the water level is at least 1 inch above the jars, and add the lids. Boil for ten minutes, remove from heat, and cool.

Pickled Turnips

مخللة

M'chalala

Turnips are used in many dishes: pickled as in this recipe, stuffed with rice and meat, or boiled overnight with tea bags and honey and served hot in the morning.

¼ cup cider vinegar	8 large turnips, halved and sliced ½ inch
1 tablespoon salt	thick
1 teaspoon lemon crystal	1 large beet, diced

Sanitize the jars (see page 39).

In a bowl combine the turnips and beets, and transfer them to the jars.

In a second large bowl, combine 6 cups of water with the vinegar, salt, and lemon crystal. Pour the mixture into the jars and seal. Keep at room temperature for 3 days to allow turnips to pickle, then refrigerate. Pickled turnips keep 6 months.

Pickled Mixed Vegetables

طرشى مخلؤط

Turshee Muchlute

Green chile peppers are used in many recipes. In particular, New Mexico or Anaheim green chile peppers are well suited for Jewish-Iraqi cuisine. They are of mild to medium hotness, 5 to 7 inches long, and 1 to 1½ inches wide. Alternately, for a hotter and spicier effect, one can use jalapeño green chiles instead.

---

1 cup balsamic vinegar

10 cloves garlic

1 teaspoon turmeric

2 teaspoons curry powder

1 teaspoon cumin

¼ cup salt

1 teaspoon ground ginger

1 teaspoon black pepper

1 teaspoon paprika

15 cardamom seeds

1 tablespoon lemon crystal

1 head (1 pound) cauliflower, cut into large pieces

4 large carrots, peeled and sliced ½ inch thick

5 fresh green chile peppers, stemmed and halved

4 zucchini, sliced crosswise 3 inches thick

Sanitize the jars (see page 39).

Place the balsamic vinegar, garlic, turmeric, curry, cumin, salt, ginger, black pepper, paprika, cardamom, and lemon crystal in a large bowl with 8 cups of water, and mix. Add the cauliflower, carrots, kohlrabi, green chile peppers, zucchini, and mix well. Transfer the mixture to the jars and seal. Keep at room temperature for 3 days to allow vegetables to pickle, then refrigerate.

Pickled vegetables keep 6 months.

Pickled Cucumbers

خيار طرشى
Chyar Turshee

MAKES 2 (16-OUNCE) JARS

Pickled cucumbers are extremely simple to make. They are a popular favorite and keep for many weeks.

1 cup wine vinegar	*1 tablespoon lemon crystal*
½ cup chopped fresh dill	*2 pounds kirby cucumbers*
¼ cup salt	*10 garlic cloves*

Sanitize the jars (see page 39).

Combine the vinegar, dill, salt, and lemon crystal in a bowl with 4 cups of water. Add the cucumbers, and garlic. Transfer the mixture to the glass jars and seal. Keep at room temperature for 3 days to allow cucumbers to pickle, then refrigerate.

Pickled Lemon

عمبة أبليمؤن

Ambah ab Lemon

Pickled lemon is distinguished by a strong acidic taste and spices that add to the flavor. Once you try it, you will want to eat more. It can be served with any main course, but it is especially good for a meal of fish on a bed of rice.

¼ cup salt	1 teaspoon black pepper
1 tablespoon turmeric	1 tablespoon paprika
1 tablespoon curry powder	½ teaspoon red pepper flakes
1 tablespoon lemon crystal	10 unpeeled lemons, sliced ½ inch thick
1 tablespoon ground ginger	10 garlic cloves, sliced

Sanitize the jars (see page 39).

In a bowl combine the salt, turmeric, curry, lemon crystal, ginger, black pepper, paprika, and red pepper with 3 cups of water and set aside for 15 minutes. Add lemon and garlic to this spice mixture and mix well. Pour into the jars, seal and keep at room temperature for 3 days to allow the lemon to pickle, then refrigerate. Pickled lemon lasts 6 months.

Soup

מרקים

مرق

Marag

Soups are very popular in Jewish Iraqi cuisine.
They can be prepared with vegetables, rice, meat,
and a wide variety of spices, served warm in the
winter and cool in the summer—frequently
cooked in large pots and later served with fresh
bread for snacks or quick meals.
Traditionally soups are used as
sources of nourishment for the
young, the elderly and the ill.
My mother as a healer cooked a
variety of soups to enhance the
strength of the weak.

Chicken Soup

مرق أبجيج

Marag ab Gige

Soups are served on all occasions, especially for holidays. Traditionally, chicken soup is prepared for Friday evening to honor the *Shabbat*.

2 teaspoons vegetable oil	½ teaspoon black pepper
1 small onion, chopped	½ teaspoon dried oregano
2 pounds chicken breast, diced	½ teaspoon red pepper flakes
½ cup chopped fresh cilantro	1 (4 ounces) can tomato sauce
2 stalks celery, chopped	Juice of 1 large lemon
8 garlic cloves, sliced	1 cup (about 12 small) sliced button
½ teaspoon salt	mushrooms
1 teaspoon curry powder	

Heat the vegetable oil in a large pot and add the onion. Stir in the chicken, cilantro, celery, and garlic, over high heat for 1 minute. Reduce heat to medium. Stir in the salt, curry, black pepper, oregano, red pepper, tomato sauce, and lemon juice, plus 6 cups of water, and bring to a boil. Reduce heat to low. Cover and cook until chicken is tender (about ½ hour). Remove from heat and add the mushrooms. Serve hot.

"*Mah yitchalat, mah yitmalach*" ("He neither mixes nor shares his salt") refers to a person who isolates himself from others. He is like food without salt.

Chicken and Rice Soup

شـؤربة
Shorba

Shorba is prepared in the winter. Its cultural significance is explained by the expression following this recipe.

2 teaspoons vegetable oil	1 teaspoon ground turmeric
2 medium-size onions, diced	½ teaspoon black pepper
1½ pounds chicken breast, diced	½ teaspoon ground ginger
6 cloves garlic, sliced	¼ teaspoon ground cloves
¾ uncooked cup rice	¼ cup (2 tablespoons) chopped fresh mint
1 (8-ounce) can tomato sauce	
½ teaspoon salt	

Heat the vegetable oil in a large pot and add the onion. Add the chicken and garlic over high heat and stir for a minute, then add the rice, and stir again. Reduce heat to medium. Add the tomato sauce, 6 cups of water, mix, and bring to a boil. Add the salt, turmeric, black pepper, ginger, and cloves, and stir. Reduce heat to low. Cover and simmer until chicken and rice are tender (about ½ an hour). Remove from heat, add the mint, stir and serve hot.

Potato Soup

مرق أبطأطأ
Marag ab Pateta

Jewish Iraqis use all kinds of potatoes in their cuisine. They use whatever is available. Therefore, any kind of potato is suitable for this recipe. Potato soup is very light and easy to digest. It is usually served with fresh bread and pickles, hot in the winter and at room temperature in the summer.

2 teaspoons olive oil	½ teaspoon cumin powder
1 cup (about 8) chopped scallions	½ teaspoon curry powder
1 stalk celery, chopped	Juice from 1 large lemon
8 large potatoes, peeled and diced	½ teaspoon black pepper
1 tablespoon chicken bouillon powder	½ teaspoon ground ginger
1 tablespoon dried dill	
½ teaspoon salt	1 cup chopped fresh spinach

Heat the olive oil in a large pot and add the scallions. Add the celery and stir for 2 minutes over high heat. Add the potatoes, chicken bouillon, and 6 cups of water, stir, and bring to a boil. Reduce heat to medium. Stir in the dill, salt, cumin, curry, lemon juice, black pepper, and ginger. Reduce heat to low. Cover and simmer until potatoes are tender (about 20 minutes). Remove from heat and stir in the spinach. Serve hot or cold.

Lentil Soup

مرق أبعدس

Marag ab Adass

The flavor of this soup is delicately enhanced by spices and rice. The soup is generally served in the winter time and accompanied by bread and pickles.

2 teaspoons olive oil	½ teaspoon ground turmeric
1 small onion, chopped	1 uncooked cup rice
1 stalk celery, chopped	1 cup dried green lentils, rinsed
1 teaspoon salt	1 cup dried orange lentils, rinsed
½ teaspoon garlic powder	3 large tomatoes, minced
½ teaspoon black pepper	½ cup (about 4) chopped scallions
1 teaspoon ground cumin	¼ cup (2 tablespoons) chopped fresh mint

Heat the olive oil in a large pot and add the onion. Add the celery, salt, garlic, black pepper, cumin, and turmeric, and stir for 1 minute over high heat. Add the rice, lentils, and tomatoes. Reduce heat to medium, add 8 cups of water, and bring to a boil. Reduce heat to low. Cover and simmer until rice and lentils are tender (about ½ hour). Remove from heat. Stir in the scallions and mint, and serve hot.

"*Sh'rubo ala kad haltoo*" ("Let him drink as much as he can tolerate") means that one should allow a person to do what he is capable of doing, without pushing him beyond his ability.

Beef, Zucchini and Leek Soup

مرق أبلحم وؤكؤوسأ

Marag ab Lahm oo Koossa

This soup, rich with vegetables, meat, spices, lemon juice, and herbs, is often eaten as a meal. It is served with a side dish of rice, or with bread and pickles.

2 teaspoons vegetable oil	½ dried dill
1 small onion, chopped	½ teaspoon curry powder
1 pound lean stew beef, cubed	½ teaspoon ground ginger
2 stalks celery, chopped	4 large zucchini, diced
1 (4-ounces) can tomato sauce	2 leek, well-rinsed and chopped
Juice of 1 large lemon	1 green bell pepper, chopped
½ teaspoon salt	2 large tomatoes, minced
½ teaspoon garlic powder	½ cup (about 4) chopped scallions
½ teaspoon black pepper	¼ cup chopped fresh parsley

Heat the vegetable oil over high heat in a large pot and add the onion. Add the meat and stir for 2 minutes over high heat. Reduce heat to medium. Add the celery, 5 cups of water, tomato sauce, lemon juice, salt, garlic, black pepper, dill, curry, and ginger, and bring to a boil. Reduce heat to low, cover and simmer until the beef is tender (about 20 minutes). Add the zucchini, leek, and bell pepper, and simmer for an additional 10 minutes. Remove from heat and stir in the tomatoes, scallions, and parsley. Serve hot.

One Way Out

*A*fter years of persecution, an Iraqi law of *Tasqueet*, which permitted Jewish immigration to Israel, was issued in 1950. A *Tasqueet* center was opened for whose who wished to leave, provided they renounce their citizenship and leave their birth certificates and all possessions behind. We were allowed to take nothing except the clothes we were wearing. My parents signed the *Tasqueet* agreement, and left their life in Basra behind. We were issued laissez-passer emigration passports with no return.

The eldest of the four remaining children, I carried my three-month-old brother in my arms. My other two siblings hung onto my dress, when we were separated from our parents and led into a large room. We were stripped completely naked and inspected for money or jewels. When neither was found, we were allowed to dress, and were directed to march toward a small plane in the middle of a field, with a ladder attached to it. I was only seven years old and had never seen an airplane before. I watched my siblings and held my baby brother tightly. I was not told my parents' whereabouts, just to board the airplane. We climbed the ladder, the baby and myself behind my siblings, who were reassured that I was there with them. When we reached the final step, I felt that my heart had stopped beating, for the space between the last step and the plane seemed so large that I feared would I fall and drop the baby. I reached my leg as far out as I could, when suddenly I felt the two large arms of the steward lift me up into the air and place me on the safe floor of the craft. Just as we were seated, my parents boarded the plane. With relief I gave them my baby brother and sat with my sister, forgetting my fear.

It was only a short while after the plane took off that we heard shouting, and saw a woman escorted to the captain's cabin. She had been caught smuggling money. She had made an inner layer in her jacket and put a large amount of money inside. Escaping the inspection, she could not contain her excitement and had advertised her wisdom out loud, so that the stewardess could hear. The money was taken, but her life was spared.

We arrived in Tel Aviv and were taken to a very large camp with many other Iraqi Jews. We were soon united with my older brothers and our extended family, and moved to live in Jerusalem. There I grew up, roaming meadows and mountains, a free person in her own homeland.

Egg Dishes

ביצים

تحلُريج

Teharige

The names of some of the recipes included
here are present in other Middle Eastern
cuisines, but the recipes themselves are unique to
Iraqi Jews, and some are unique to my family.

Feta Cheese Omelets

عجة أبجبن
Aja ab Jibin

Feta is the most frequently used cheese in Jewish-Iraqi cuisine. One of my fond childhood memories is of afternoon tea, served with fresh bread and feta cheese. *Aja* makes a quick, light meal, especially when stuffed in pita with a mixed salad and pickles.

4 eggs, lightly beaten	*¼ teaspoon black pepper*
8 ounces feta cheese, crumbled	*1 large clove garlic, minced*
¼ teaspoon white pepper	*2 teaspoons vegetable oil*

Pour the eggs into a bowl, and stir in the feta cheese, white pepper, black pepper, and garlic.

Heat the oil in a skillet over high heat. Reduce heat to medium. Drop in tablespoons of the egg mixture and fry until it is golden brown on both sides.

Alternately, pour all the egg mixture into the pan, and spread it evenly with a spatula. Reduce heat to low. Cover and cook until no liquid remains on top of the mixture (about 5 minutes). Uncover, flip the omelet, and cook until golden brown on both sides.

Brown Eggs and Vegetables

تحأريج ملشبأث
Teharige mal Shubath

All of our meals are prepared on Friday and cooked with low heat overnight so they can be served warm on Saturday, our day of rest. Traditionally, breakfast for this day is brown eggs. The eggs are served with many side ingredients as listed below. Although my husband and our children were born in the USA, *teharige mal Shubath* (Sabbath eggs) is their favorite breakfast.

10 eggs	1 cup (about 10) sliced radishes
3 black tea bags	1 cup olives
10 pita breads, white or whole wheat	1 cup (8 ounce jar) pepperoncini
Pickled mango (page 39)	1 cup fresh parsley, stemmed
Fried eggplant (page 72)	1 cup fresh mint or basil, stemmed
Mixed salad (page 19)	

Preheat the oven to 200°F.

Put 5 cups of water, eggs, and tea bags in an ovenproof pan. Place in the oven overnight (about 10 to 12 hours).

Serve the eggs hot in pita bread as follows; slice one egg, open the pita to form a pocket, spread 1 tablespoon of the pickled mangoes inside, then add the egg, fried eggplant, salad, radishes, olive, and pepperoncini. Top with parsley, and mint or basil leaves.

Eggs with Meat

تحلريج بلحم
Teharige ab Lahm

This dish is easily prepared from leftover meat or chicken. If the meat is not ground, it should be finely chopped. Leftover green vegetables and rice can be added as well, changing an old dish into a new one.

3 eggs, lightly beaten	½ teaspoon salt
4 ounces ground lean beef or chicken, or	½ teaspoon garlic powder
1 cup chopped leftover meat	½ teaspoon ground ginger
½ cup (about 4) chopped scallions	Juice from 1 large lemon
2 fresh leeks, well-rinsed and chopped	2 teaspoons olive oil

Combine the eggs, beef, scallions, leeks, salt, garlic powder, ginger, and lemon juice in a bowl. Heat the olive oil in a skillet over high heat. Reduce heat to low. Pour the meat mixture into the pan and spread it evenly with a spatula. Cover and cook until no liquid remains on top of the mixture (about 5 minutes). Uncover, flip the omelet, and cook until golden brown on both sides.

"When yaphra haphi baitha" ("stop or end up like an empty shell") refers to an addictive gambler who, having lost his money, is like an eggshell without nutrients within it.

Spiced Eggs with Onion

تحلﺭﻴﺞ أببصﻞ
Teharige ab Bassal

3 SERVINGS

This combination of onion, mint, cilantro, chives, eggs, and spices makes for a delightful flavor and fragrance. This dish can be served as an hors d'oeuvre, or eaten with salad, olives, and pickles as a light meal.

3 eggs, lightly beaten	½ teaspoon curry powder
2 medium-size onions, chopped	½ teaspoon black pepper
¼ cup chopped fresh cilantro	½ teaspoon garlic powder
¼ cup chopped fresh mint	Juice of 1 small lemon
2 tablespoons chopped chives	2 teaspoons olive oil
½ teaspoon salt	

In a bowl combine the eggs, onions, cilantro, mint, chives, salt, curry, black pepper, garlic powder, and lemon juice.

Heat the olive oil in a skillet over high heat. Reduce heat to low. Pour the egg mixture into the pan and spread evenly with a spatula. Cover and cook until no liquid remains on top of the mixture (about 5 minutes). Uncover, flip the omelet, and cook until golden brown on both sides.

Mama Nazima's Jewish-Iraqi Cuisine

Eggs and Vegetables

שקשוקה
Shakshuka

My family likes the eggs scrambled with the vegetables because they take on a creamy texture. Others prefer to cook the eggs with the vegetables without breaking the yolks.

3 eggs, lightly beaten	½ teaspoon garlic powder
2 medium-size onions, sliced	½ teaspoon ground ginger
2 large tomatoes, chopped	½ teaspoon curry powder
¼ cup chopped fresh parsley	Juice of 1 small lemon
¼ cup chopped fresh basil or mint	½ teaspoon paprika
¼ cup chopped fresh green chile peppers	2 teaspoons vegetable oil
½ teaspoon salt	

Combine the eggs, onions, tomatoes, parsley, basil, chile peppers, salt, garlic powder, ginger, curry, lemon juice, and paprika in a bowl. Heat the vegetable oil in a skillet over high heat. Reduce heat to low. Pour the egg mixture into the pan, cook, stirring occasionally, until no liquid remains (about 5 minutes). Serve hot.

Stuffed Eggs

Stuffed eggs are extremely popular, especially with children. In my parents' home, my siblings and I participated in the preparation of this dish. My mother did the sautéing, and we enjoyed stuffing the eggs and later eating them while they were still warm.

8 eggs, hard-boiled and shelled	*¼ cup chopped fresh parsley*
2 teaspoons olive oil	*½ teaspoon salt*
1 small onion, chopped	*½ teaspoon garlic powder*
1 stalk celery, chopped	*Juice of 1 small lemon*
1 large tomato, chopped	*½ teaspoon ground ginger*
½ cup (about 6 small) chopped button	*½ teaspoon paprika*
mushrooms	*¼ cup chopped fresh parsley*

Half the eggs and remove the yolks carefully so they do not break or crumble, and set aside.

Heat the olive oil in a skillet over high heat and add the onion. Reduce heat to low. Add the celery and tomato, and stir until the celery is semi-cooked (about 3 minutes). Stir in the mushrooms, salt, garlic, lemon juice, ginger, and paprika. Remove from heat.

Stuff each egg white half with the onion mixture, and top each with half an egg yolk. Place the eggs on a platter and garnish with the parsley.

Eggs Scrambled with Matzoh

تحلأريج أبمصة
Teharige ab Mazza

This meal is traditionally prepared for the Passover holiday, which celebrates the Jews' exodus from Egypt, the land of bondage, to Israel, the land of freedom. Matzoh, which resemble large crackers, are made from unleavened dough and baked in sheets about 8 inches square.

½ cup milk	Juice of 1 large lemon
4 matzoh, crumbled	¼ teaspoon ginger, ground
4 eggs lightly beaten	¼ teaspoon paprika
½ teaspoon salt	2 teaspoons vegetable oil
½ teaspoon garlic powder	

Put milk and the matzoh in a bowl. Let the matzoh soak up the milk for 1 minute. Pour the eggs over the matzoh. Stir in the salt, garlic, lemon juice, ginger, and paprika.

Heat the oil in a skillet over high heat. Reduce heat to low, pour in the matzoh mixture and spread evenly with a spatula. Cook and stir occasionally until golden brown.

Lentils, Tomatoes, and Eggs

شر ؤبر

Shure oo Bure

This dish is generally prepared in the winter because it is served hot and is highly nutritious. Additionally, lentils, tomatoes, and eggs are available year round. Served with fresh bread and pickles, they make for a hearty meal.

1½ cups dried orange lentils
2 teaspoons vegetable oil
2 medium-size onions, chopped
1 (4-ounce) can tomato sauce
½ teaspoon salt
½ teaspoon garlic powder

½ teaspoon black pepper
½ teaspoon ground cumin
½ teaspoon hot paprika
2 large tomatoes, minced
4 eggs

Rinse the lentils and drain. Heat the vegetable oil in a pan over high heat and add the onions. Cook until lightly browned. Reduce heat to medium, stir in the lentils, and cook for 2 minutes. Stir in the tomato sauce, salt, garlic, black pepper, cumin, paprika, and 3 cups of water, and bring to a boil. Stir in the minced tomatoes. Reduce heat to low. Crack the eggs into the lentil mixture. Do not break the yolks and do not stir. Cover and simmer until the lentils are tender (about ½ hour). Serve hot.

Cauliflower, Bell Peppers

تحلَّريج أبقرنبط وَفلفل

Teharige ab Karnabit oo Filfil

Cauliflower is used in many Jewish-Iraqi dishes. My sister-in-law Daisy taught me that when cooking cauliflower, one should keep a corner of the pan uncovered to let the gases escape. If they do not escape, they are absorbed in the cauliflower, making it difficult to digest.

1 pound (1 head) cauliflower, chopped	½ teaspoon dried oregano
1 green bell pepper, chopped	½ teaspoon black pepper
1 red bell pepper, chopped	½ teaspoon hot paprika
1 medium-size onion, chopped	½ teaspoon ground ginger
½ cup (about 4) chopped scallions	¼ teaspoon ground cloves
½ cup chopped fresh basil	4 eggs, lightly beaten
2 large tomatoes, minced	2 tablespoons all-purpose flour
½ teaspoon salt	2 teaspoons olive oil
½ teaspoon garlic powder	

Combine the cauliflower, green and red bell peppers, onion, scallions, basil, and tomatoes in a bowl. Stir in the salt, garlic powder, oregano, black pepper, paprika, ginger, and cloves. Pour the eggs over the vegetables, add the flour, and mix well.

Heat the olive oil in a pan over high heat. Reduce heat to low. Then drop tablespoons of the egg mixture into the pan and fry until golden brown on both sides.

Alternately, pour all the egg mixture into the pan, and spread it evenly with a spatula. Reduce heat to low. Cover and cook until no liquid remains on top of the mixture (about 5 minutes). Uncover, flip the omelet, and cook until golden brown on both sides.

Vegetarian Dishes

ירקות

خضأر

Chuthrawat

Vegetables are one of the most important items
in the Jewish Iraqi diet. In Israel, cauliflower,
peppers, and cabbage are plentiful in the winter.
Cucumbers, fresh beans, and squash can be found
easily in spring and summer and eggplant and
tomatoes are abundant for almost the entire year.

Butternut Squash and Apricots

طرشأنة

Tershana

Holidays are celebrated with many foods, some of which are seasonal. For *Tu Bishvat*, the "holiday of trees," which occurs in early spring, it is customary to eat dried fruit and nuts. *Tershana*, which includes these nourishing items, is served with rice.

2 teaspoons vegetable oil	1 teaspoon curry powder
1 large onion, diced	½ teaspoon paprika
1 (8-ounces) can tomato sauce	4 tablespoons lemon juice
1 large butternut squash, peeled and cubed	2 tablespoons honey
	1 cup dried apricots
½ teaspoon salt	⅔ cup raisins
½ teaspoon garlic powder	1 cup whole almonds
½ teaspoon black pepper	

Heat the vegetable oil in a large pot over high heat and add the onions. Reduce heat to medium. Add the tomato sauce, 1 cup of water, squash, salt, garlic, black pepper, curry, and paprika, and bring the mixture to a boil. Add the lemon juice and honey, cover and cook until the squash is tender (about 10 minutes). Reduce heat to low and add the apricots, raisins, and almonds. Simmer for an additional 5 minutes. Serve hot or cold.

Okra, Garlic, and Mint

بأمية أبثّوم وُنعناع

Bamia ab Thum oo Nanah

Traditionally, *bamia* is served once a week, hot or cold on a bed of rice. My mother always cooked a big pot of it so there would be plenty left over, because we loved it even more when it was cold. Iraqi Jews eat it almost year round.

2 teaspoons vegetable oil	½ teaspoon red pepper flakes
1 small onion, chopped	½ teaspoon ground ginger
2 pounds okra, chopped	½ teaspoon paprika
1 (8-ounce) can tomato sauce	Juice 1 of large lemon
10 garlic cloves, sliced	1 tablespoon sugar or honey
½ teaspoon salt	½ cup chopped fresh mint
½ teaspoon black pepper	

Heat the oil in a pot over high heat and add the onion. Add the okra, tomato sauce, and 2 cups of water, and bring to a boil. Reduce heat to medium. Cover and cook until the okra is semi-tender (about 10 minutes). Reduce heat to low and add the garlic, salt, black pepper, red pepper, ginger, and paprika. Cover and simmer until the okra is tender (about 15 minutes). Stir in the lemon juice, sugar, and mint, and simmer for additional 10 minutes.

Black-Eyed Peas

لوبيا مسلوقة
Lubia Muslukah

8 SERVINGS

Black-eyed peas are one of the symbolic foods consumed at the New Year. It is customary to bless the peas to bring many great events and avoid disastrous ones. This dish is also prepared in the winter. Serve it hot with lemon juice.

2 teaspoons olive oil	½ teaspoon garlic powder
1 medium-size onion, chopped	½ teaspoon dried rosemary
2 pounds fresh black-eyed peas	¼ teaspoon dried sage
½ teaspoon salt	Juice of 1 large lemon
½ teaspoon black pepper	

Heat the olive oil in a pot over high heat, add the onion and black-eyed peas to 2½ cups of water, and bring to a boil. Cook until the peas are semitender (about 10 minutes). Stir in the salt, black pepper, garlic powder, rosemary, and sage. Cover and reduce heat to medium and cook until the peas are tender (about 10 minutes). Reduce heat to low, add the lemon juice, and simmer for an additional 10 minutes. Serve hot or cold.

"Akale balah eyen" ("Eating without seeing") refers to one who is so hungry, that even the type of food he eats does not matter.

Potatoes and Fried Eggplant

بطأطأ ؤيأبنجأن مقلى

Pateta oo Babinjan Mukli

This combination of potato and fried eggplant makes a great side dish. It can be also served with sliced feta cheese, sliced tomato, pickles, and fresh bread.

1 large eggplant, peeled and sliced ¼ inch thick	*½ teaspoon garlic powder*
1½ teaspoons salt	*½ teaspoon black pepper*
1 tablespoon vegetable oil	*¼ cup chopped fresh basil*
6 large potatoes, peeled, sliced ¼ inch thick, and steamed	*¼ cup chopped fresh mint*

Sprinkle 1 teaspoon of the salt over the eggplant, and set aside for 1 hour. Gently squeeze the eggplant to remove any liquid. Heat the vegetable oil over medium heat and fry the eggplant until golden brown on both sides. Transfer to paper towels to soak up the oil.

Combine the remaining ½ teaspoon of the salt, garlic, and black pepper in a small bowl. Sprinkle the spices over the potatoes. Arrange the potatoes and eggplant slices on a platter and sprinkle with the basil and mint. Serve hot or cold.

72
Mama Nazima's Jewish-Iraqi Cuisine

Fried Tomatoes

طمأطأ مقلية
Tamata Muklyee

This dish, served hot or cold, is mostly eaten in the summer, when tomatoes are readily available. The aroma of the spices blends with the taste of the fried tomatoes to make an exquisite meal of delicate flavor. The color of the tomatoes and the spices adds to the presentation and enhances one's appetite.

2 teaspoons olive oil	¼ teaspoon paprika
4 large tomatoes, halved	¼ teaspoon dried oregano
¼ teaspoon salt	½ cup (about 4) chopped scallions
¼ teaspoon garlic powder	

Heat the olive oil in a pan over a high heat. Reduce heat to low and place the tomatoes, cut side up, in the pan. Combine the salt, garlic powder, paprika, and oregano in a small bowl. Sprinkle the spice mixture over the tomatoes and cook until the tomatoes are semi-tender (about 3 minutes).

Remove from heat, arrange on a platter, and garnish with the chopped scallions.

String Beans

لؤبياً خضراً

Lubia Chuthra

My mother always cautioned me not to overcook vegetables. I remember her saying, "*El mona malo etruh*" ("They lose their nutrients"). String beans need to be tender but not mushy.

3 pounds string beans, trimmed	*½ teaspoon ground ginger*
1 medium-size kohlrabi, chopped	*½ teaspoon black pepper*
½ teaspoon salt	*Juice of 1 large lemon*
½ teaspoon paprika	*2 teaspoons olive oil*
½ teaspoon garlic powder	*½ cup (about 4) chopped scallions*
½ teaspoon dried oregano	

Steam the beans until tender (about 20 minutes). Remove from heat and cool.

Combine the kohlrabi, salt, paprika, garlic powder, oregano, ginger, black pepper, lemon juice, olive oil, and scallions in a bowl. Add the kohlrabi mixture to the string beans and mix. Serve cold.

Kidney Beans, Scallions and Chile

أرحم أبيؤل

Lubia Hamra

If you wish to use dried kidney beans, you need to start the night prior to the preparation of the main part of this meal. Allowing the beans to soak in water makes it faster to cook them. Alternately, you may replace the dried beans with canned of beans.

3 cups dried kidney beans, or 2 (15-ounce) can	½ teaspoon black pepper
2 teaspoons olive oil	6 bay leaves
1 cup (about 8) chopped scallions	½ teaspoon paprika
½ cup chopped small green chile peppers	1 (8-ounce) can tomato sauce
¼ cup chopped fresh cilantro	Juice of 2 large lemons
4 garlic cloves, crushed	1 large tomato, minced
1 teaspoon salt	

Put the dried beans in a bowl and cover with water. Leave overnight to soften. Then rinse beans and drain. If using canned beans, drain and rinse.

Heat the olive oil in a pot over high heat and add ½ cup of the scallions. Stir in the chile, cilantro, garlic, and beans. Add 4 cups of water and bring to a boil. Stir in the salt, black pepper, bay leaves, and paprika. Reduce heat to medium. Cover

and cook until the beans are tender (about ½ hour). Add the tomato sauce and 1 cup of water and simmer for 10 minutes. Remove from heat, and add the lemon juice, tomatoes, and the remaining ½ cup of the scallions. Serve hot or cold.

Fried Vegetables

خضره مقلية

Chuthar Muklyee

8 SERVINGS

This dish is served with Brown Eggs (page 58) for the *Shabbat* brunch. Since the *Shabbat* is a day of rest, and no cooking is done on this day, the vegetables are prepared the day before. They are also cooked for other special occasions. They are served with lemon juice and sprinkled with parsley and mint.

1 large eggplant, peeled and cut into ¼ inch slices	*2 large zucchini, trimmed and sliced lengthwise into 8 pieces*
1 large butternut squash, peeled and cut into ¼ inch slices	*2 green bell peppers, seeded and sliced lengthwise into 8 pieces*
2 teaspoons salt	*2 red bell peppers, seeded and sliced lengthwise into 8 pieces*
3 tablespoons vegetable oil	

Sprinkle 1 teaspoon of the salt over the eggplant, and the remaining teaspoon of the salt over the squash and set aside in separate colanders for 1 hour, or put them into one colander without mixing them.

Gently squeeze the eggplant to remove any liquid and set on a large plate. Dry the squash with paper towels to remove any liquid and set on a second large plate.

Heat 1 tablespoon of the vegetable oil in a skillet over a high heat. Then reduce heat to medium, fry the eggplant until golden brown on both sides, and transfer to paper towels to soak up the oil.

In the same skillet, fry the squash with 1 tablespoon of the remaining oil over medium heat until golden brown, and transfer to paper towels to soak up the oil. Then in the same skillet, fry the zucchini and peppers with the remaining 1 tablespoon of oil over medium heat until golden brown on both sides. Transfer to paper towels to soak up the oil. Arrange the fried vegetables neatly on a platter. Serve cold.

Mama Nazima's Jewish-Iraqi Cuisine

Fava Beans

بَاقِلَى
Bakili

Fava beans are one of the most favorite Jewish-Iraqi dishes. They are also known as broad beans and can be found in Middle Eastern shops, fresh, dried, canned, or frozen. If you wish to use frozen fava beans, you must thoroughly defrost them and drain off the water. Olive oil, lemon juice, herbs, and spices give a great flavor to this dish.

1 pound dried fava beans (see Note)	*½ teaspoon black pepper*
1 teaspoon salt	*¼ cup chopped fresh parsley*
	¼ cup chopped fresh mint
DRESSING:	*¼ cup fresh chopped small green chile*
Juice of 1 large lemon	*peppers*
½ teaspoon garlic powder	*2 teaspoons olive oil*

Put the fava beans in a bowl and cover with water. Leave overnight to soften. Then rinse the beans and put them in a pot. Add 6 cups of water, and the salt, and bring to a boil over high heat. Reduce heat to medium. Cover and cook until the beans become tender (about 40 minutes). Drain, cool, peel, mash and place in a serving bowl.

DRESSING:
Combine the lemon juice, garlic powder, black pepper, parsley, mint, and green chile peppers in a small bowl. Stir in the olive oil. Stir the dressing into the mashed fava beans. Chill and serve.

NOTE: CAUTION—Do not serve fava beans to people who are known to be allergic to fava beans or have G6PD deficiency. It can lead to severe, life-threatening anemia and is inherited; people are born with it.

G6PD deficiency is common in people from the Mediterranean area of Asia, especially Northern Iraq and Syria. Also, in the United States, ten per cent of African-American males have a deficiency of this enzyme.

Potatoes with Cilantro

بطأطأ أبكزبغة

Pateta ab Koossbara

This dish was created by my mother. Since her children and grandchildren were potato lovers, she cooked the potatoes (any kind of potato can be used) with onions, cilantro, and spices to give them a great taste and add color to the presentation of the dish.

5 large potatoes, peeled, cubed, and steamed	½ teaspoon garlic powder
2 teaspoons olive oil	½ teaspoon black pepper
1 small onion, chopped	½ teaspoon dried oregano
½ cup chopped fresh cilantro	juice of 1 large lemon
½ teaspoon salt	1 cup (about 8) chopped scallions

Place the potatoes in a bowl.

Heat the olive oil in a skillet over high heat and add the onion and cilantro. Reduce heat to low. Stir in the salt, garlic powder, black pepper, oregano, and lemon juice for 1 minute. Remove from heat and add the scallions.

Stir the onion mixture into the potatoes. Transfer to a platter. Serve hot or cold.

Kidnapped

There was a woman in Basra, who prayed every day to have a little girl to hold and dress with pretty clothing so that she would look like a princess. She already had three sons and loved them dearly, but still she yearned for a daughter.

One day as she was walking and drifting in her thoughts, she came upon a temple without realizing where she was. Inspired by chance, she entered and prayed. "Dear God! If you grant me a girl, I will dress her with a dress as beautiful and colorful as a rainbow. On each month, on the day of her birth, I will buy an expensive jewel and pin it to her dress. When my girl reaches a year old, I will donate all the jewels to the temple."

One year later her wish was granted, and she gave birth to a baby girl. As she had sworn, she dressed her newborn daughter in a multihued dress, and as the baby grew, she added other pieces of cloth to make the dress bigger. So, as promised, the baby was wearing a rainbow dress, and each month the mother bought an expensive jewel and pinned it to the baby's dress.

On the day when the baby reached 10 months of age, the mother left her with the nanny and went to buy another jewel. The baby began to cry, and as much as the nanny tried to quiet her, it was to no avail. The nanny decided to walk the baby outside; perhaps this would calm her down. Once outside, an Iraqi woman heard the baby's cry and came to the nanny. She asked why the baby was crying. "She wants her mother," the nanny answered. "Give me the baby. Here, take this money and buy her candy," said the seemingly benevolent Iraqi woman. The nanny, excited by the prospect of soothing the child's tears, took the money, and rushed to buy candy from a nearby vendor. As soon as she turned her head, the woman had vanished with the baby, and both were nowhere to be found.

Upon hearing the news, the little girl's parents were devastated. Since her father had friends in the local police department, they were called, and the search began. A police jeep with a loudspeaker drove through the town, describing the baby and announcing a generous reward for her safe return. Many people gathered, and many more marched behind the police car.

The sun began to set when a garbage truck drove by the crowd. "What is happening?" asked the driver. He was told that a child had been kidnapped. As soon as he heard this, he informed the police that he had found an infant girl in the garbage dump outside of the city. "The baby was naked and was crying. I thought that she belonged to the Bedouins who lived near the dump. I gave the baby to the Bedouin woman." He went on, describing the place where the Bedouins set their tents.

With a breath of hope, the baby's parents and the police raced toward the Bedouin camp. As the car sped on, a sudden fear overwhelmed the mother. "What if night falls? What if the campsite cannot be found in the dark?" she thought. As she watched the sun move down toward the horizon, she began to pray, "Please

God! Don't let the sun set. Let there be light until we reach the Bedouin camp." With racing hearts, they found the Bedouin tents before nightfall. Miraculously, much to their relief, they saw their baby sleeping peacefully, dressed in Bedouin clothing, fed and cared for. A Bedouin woman had cared for the strange, unknown baby and treated her like her own.

The kidnapped baby, who was returned safely to her parents with neither her jewels nor her rainbow dress, was me, the author of this book. I have always wondered what would have become of me had my parents not be able to find me. Probably I would have become a Bedouin woman, never knowing my true heritage.

When I had a chance to work with Bedouins in the Sinai Peninsula, I did not hesitate despite the danger, because they had once saved my life. When I worked with them and learned about their culture and their ancient medicine, I grew to love them for their wisdom and simplicity.

Meat Dishes

בשר

لحم

Lahm

Iraqi Jews use various types of meat, including beef, veal, lamb, chicken, and turkey. Most of the meat dishes are cooked with a variety of vegetables. We use ground beef, chicken, or turkey for such favorite meals as dumplings, stuffed vegetables, and stuffed meat.

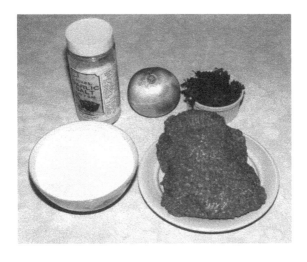

Eggplant with Meat

إنكرى أبلحم وُجيج

Engreyee ab Lahm oo Gige

Engreyee is always made with fried eggplant, whose texture and flavor complement the accompanying meat and vegetables. When this dish is blended with the spices, the aroma is enhanced during both the cooking and the serving.

1 large eggplant, peeled and cut into ¼ inch slices	*½ teaspoon ground turmeric*
1½ teaspoons salt	*½ teaspoon red pepper flakes*
1 tablespoon vegetable oil	*½ teaspoon dried oregano*
1 (8-ounces) can tomato sauce	*½ teaspoon dried thyme*
2 medium onions, sliced	*2 large zucchini, sliced*
2 stalks celery, chopped	*3 crookneck squash, sliced*
2 large carrots, peeled and sliced	*1 cup (about 12 small) sliced button mushrooms*
2 pounds lean beef or chicken breast, cubed	*Juice of 2 large lemons*
½ teaspoon black pepper	*2 tablespoons honey*
1 teaspoon curry powder	

Sprinkle 1 teaspoon of the salt over the eggplant, and set aside for 1 hour in a colander. Gently squeeze the eggplant slices to remove any liquid. Heat the vegetable oil in a skillet over high heat, reduce heat to medium, and fry the eggplant until golden brown on both sides. Transfer to paper towels to soak up the oil.

Put the tomato sauce, 2 cups of water, onions, celery, carrots, and meat in a pot, and bring to a boil. Reduce heat to medium and stir in the remaining ½ teaspoon of the salt, and the black pepper, curry, turmeric, red pepper, oregano, and thyme. Cook until meat is tender (about 10 minutes).

Reduce heat to low, add the zucchini and simmer for 5 minutes. Add the crookneck squash and mushrooms, and simmer for 5 minutes. Stir in the fried eggplant, lemon juice, and honey, and simmer for an additional 5 minutes.

Sweet-and-Sour Okra with Meat

بأمية حلوَء أبلحم

Bamia Hulwa ab Lahm

Sweet-and-sour okra is traditionally served hot or cold over a bed of white rice. Fresh okra is preferable, but you may substitute frozen okra and thaw it before cooking.

2 teaspoons vegetable oil	*½ teaspoon paprika*
1 medium-size onion, chopped	*½ teaspoon celery seeds*
2 pounds lean beef or chicken breast,	*½ teaspoon red pepper flakes*
* cubed*	*1 teaspoon curry powder*
2 pounds fresh okra, chopped	*Juice of 1 large lemon*
1 (8-ounce) can tomato sauce	*2 tablespoons honey*
½ teaspoon salt	*4 large tomatoes, minced*
½ teaspoon black pepper	

Heat the vegetable oil in a pot over high heat and add the onion. Reduce heat to medium. Add the meat, okra, tomato sauce, and 3 cups of water, and bring to a boil. Stir in the salt, black pepper, paprika, celery seeds, red pepper, and curry. Cover and cook until meat is tender (about 20 minutes), then reduce heat to low and add the lemon juice and honey. Cover and simmer for 10 minutes. Next, add the tomatoes, and simmer for 5 additional minutes. Serve hot or cold.

Meat, Potatoes, and Zucchini

بطأطأ وَكوساً أبلحم

Pateta oo Koossa ab Lahm

Traditionally this dish is served on a bed of rice. The tomatoes are added just before serving while the dish is still hot. This heats the tomatoes without allowing them to disintegrate and adds color to the presentation.

2 teaspoons olive oil	½ teaspoon celery seeds
1 medium-size onion, chopped	½ teaspoon dried oregano
2 pounds lean beef or chicken breast, cubed	½ teaspoon garlic powder
2 large potatoes, peeled and cubed	2 large zucchini, cleaned and thickly sliced
2 large carrots, peeled and sliced	3 crookneck squash, cleaned and thickly
1 (4-ounce) can tomato sauce	sliced
½ teaspoon salt	Juice of 1 large lemon
½ teaspoon hot paprika	¼ cup chopped fresh mint
1 teaspoon curry powder	2 large tomatoes, cut into 8 pieces each
½ teaspoon ground ginger	

Heat the olive oil in a large pot over high heat, add the onion, meat, and stir for 2 minutes. Add 2½ cups of water, the potatoes, carrots, and tomato sauce, and bring to a boil. Reduce heat to medium. Cover and cook until the meat is tender (about 20 minutes). Stir in the salt, paprika, curry, ginger, celery seeds, oregano, and garlic powder. Reduce heat to low. Mix in the zucchini, cover, and simmer

for 5 minutes. Next, add the crookneck squash and lemon juice, cover and simmer for 5 minutes. Remove from heat, and add the mint and tomatoes. Serve hot.

Meat Kebabs

كباب أبلحم
Kabab ab Lahm

Kebabs are made from beef, chicken, or turkey and often served in a pita bread, stuffed with mixed salad (page 19) and pickles. Alternately, they can be served with a sauce and rice.

2 pounds lean ground beef, chicken, or turkey	**LEMON SAUCE:**
½ teaspoon salt	*2 teaspoons olive oil*
½ teaspoon black pepper	*1 small onion, chopped*
½ teaspoon red pepper flakes	*¼ cup chopped fresh cilantro*
½ teaspoon ground ginger	*Juice of 2 large lemons*
¼ teaspoon ground nutmeg	*½ teaspoon salt*
1 large onion, chopped	*½ teaspoon garlic powder*
¼ cup chopped fresh parsley	*½ teaspoon black pepper*

In a bowl combine the meat, salt, black pepper, red pepper, ginger, and nutmeg. Refrigerate for 15 minutes.

Preheat the grill over high heat.

Remove the meat from the refrigerator and stir in the onion and parsley. Divide the mixture into thirty portions, and with wet hands roll each portion into an oval shaped kebab. Put 3 kebabs on each skewer and grill, rotating occasionally, until they are crisp (about 10 minutes).

Alternately, preheat the oven at 350°F. Place the kebabs on a baking sheet and bake until they are crisp (about 20 minutes).

LEMON SAUCE:

Heat the olive oil in a pan over high heat and add the onion and cilantro. Reduce heat to low. Stir in ¾ cup of water, the lemon juice, salt, garlic, and black pepper. Bring to a boil, cover, and simmer for 5 minutes to make the sauce. Pour it over the kebabs. Serve on a bed of rice.

86   *Mama Nazima's Jewish-Iraqi Cuisine*

Meatballs and Vegetables in Tomato Sauce

كؤفتة بخضأر ؤطمأطا

Kfta ab Chuthar oo Tamata

Jewish-Iraqi cuisine includes varieties of meatballs. In every case, when you add the chopped onion and spices to the meat, you vigorously knead the mixture by hand in order to thoroughly mix it.

2 pounds lean ground beef or lamb	**SAUCE:**
1 medium-size onion, chopped	*2 teaspoons olive oil*
¼ cup chopped fresh parsley	*1 medium-size onion, chopped*
½ teaspoon salt	*1 (4-ounce) can tomato sauce*
½ teaspoon black pepper	*4 zucchini, sliced*
½ teaspoon garlic powder	*4 crookneck squash, sliced*
½ teaspoon paprika	*½ teaspoon salt*
½ teaspoon red pepper flakes	*½ teaspoon black pepper*
	Juice of 1 large lemon
	¼ teaspoon ground ginger

Using your hands, mix the meat with the onion, parsley, salt, black pepper, garlic powder, paprika, and red pepper in a bowl. With wet hands, shape into thirty balls, place on a tray, and refrigerate for ½ hour.

Heat the olive oil in a pot over high heat and add the onion. Reduce heat to medium. Add the meatballs and stir gently. Add 1½ cups of water, and the tomato sauce, and bring to a boil. Cook until the meatballs are tender (about 10 minutes). Reduce heat to low, stir in the zucchini, and cook for 5 minutes. Stir in the crookneck squash, salt, black pepper, lemon juice, and ginger. Cover and simmer for an additional 10 minutes.

Meat Patties

عرؤق أبلحم
Aurook ab Lahm

8 SERVINGS

For an attractive garnish, fry pine nuts and stick them into the top of each *aurook*.

2 pounds lean ground beef, chicken, or turkey	Juice of 1 large lemon
½ teaspoon salt	1 large onion, chopped
½ teaspoon garlic powder	¼ cup chopped fresh mint
½ teaspoon paprika	¼ cup chopped fresh cilantro
½ teaspoon red pepper flakes	1 cup cooked rice
½ teaspoon ground ginger	2 eggs, lightly beaten
½ teaspoon curry powder	2 large tomatoes, chopped
	2 teaspoons vegetable oil

Mix the meat, salt, garlic powder, paprika, red pepper, ginger, curry and lemon juice together in a large bowl. Refrigerate for 1 hour. Next add the onion, mint, cilantro, cooked rice, eggs, and tomatoes. Heat the oil in a pan over high heat, then reduce heat to low. Drop tablespoons of the meat mixture into the pan and fry until golden brown on both sides.

Alternately, brush a large pan with vegetable oil over low heat. Pour the meat mixture into the pan and spread evenly. Cover and cook until the meat is tender (about 10 minutes). Then uncover, flip the mixture, and fry until both sides are golden brown. Cut into squares.

8

Chicken, Garbanzo Beans, and Raisins

جيج أبحمص

Gige ab Hmas

Garbanzo beans and raisins are typically cooked with meat and served on a bed of rice. They also provide a special flavor to many other dishes.

½ pound dried garbanzo beans, or 1 (15-ounce) can	1½ pounds chicken breast, halved
½ teaspoon salt	2 teaspoons vegetable oil
½ teaspoon black pepper	1 medium-size onion, chopped
½ teaspoon hot paprika	1 (4-ounce) can tomato sauce
½ teaspoon garlic powder	Juice of 1 large lemon
1 teaspoon curry powder	1 cup uncooked rice
½ teaspoon ground ginger	⅔ cup raisins

If using dried beans, put the garbanzos in a bowl and cover with water. Leave overnight to soften. Then rinse the beans and set aside. If using canned, drain and rinse.

Combine the salt, black pepper, paprika, garlic powder, curry, and ginger in a small bowl. Put the chicken in a lidded container and add half the spice mixture to the chicken. Cover tightly and shake to mix the spices and the chicken. Refrigerate for ½ hour.

Preheat the oven to 350°F.

Heat the vegetable oil in a pot over high heat and add the onion, stir for 1 minute, and remove from heat.

Stir in 1½ cups of water, the tomato sauce, the lemon juice, the garbanzo beans, rice, raisins, and the remaining spice.

Transfer the bean mixture to a large baking pan. Place the chicken in the beans. Cover and bake until chicken and rice are tender (about 1 hour).

Chicken and Potatoes

جيج أبيطأطأ

Gige ab Pateta

Jewish-Iraqi cuisine puts special emphasis on preparing the meat before cooking. Spicing the meat and refrigerating it allows for absorption of the flavors, resulting in a delicious dish.

½ teaspoon salt	2 teaspoons vegetable oil
½ teaspoon black pepper	8 scallions, peeled
½ teaspoon hot paprika	1 (8-ounce) can tomato sauce
½ teaspoon dried rosemary	8 large potatoes, peeled and cubed
½ teaspoon dried oregano	¼ cup chopped fresh cilantro
½ teaspoon celery seeds	
1½ pounds chicken breast, cut to large cubes	

Combine the salt, black pepper, paprika, rosemary, oregano, and celery seeds in a bowl. Put the chicken in a lidded container and add half the spice mixture to the chicken. Cover tightly and shake well to mix with the chicken. Refrigerate for ½ hour.

Heat the vegetable oil in a pot over high heat and add the scallions. Reduce heat to medium, add the remaining spices, and mix. Stir in 2 cups of water, the tomato sauce, potatoes, and cilantro, and bring to a boil. Add the chicken, cover, and cook until the chicken is tender (about 20 minutes). Reduce heat to low and simmer for 10 more minutes.

"*Al regil gige mayi chulah*" ("Unable to untie the chicken leg") characterizes an individual who is unwilling to complete his task, or incapable of doing so.

Chicken with Almonds

8 SERVINGS

جيج أبلؤز

Gige ab Loze

The combination of almonds, raisins, and meat is often used in Jewish-Iraqi cuisine. Serve this dish on a bed of rice. The tamarind sauce is my mother's contribution, and can be found in Middle Eastern and Indian stores.

2 tablespoons tamarind sauce	1½ pounds chicken breasts, cubed
½ teaspoon salt	2 teaspoons olive oil
½ teaspoon black pepper	2 medium-size onions, sliced
½ teaspoon garlic powder	⅔ cup raisins
½ teaspoon paprika	¼ cup almonds, sliced

Preheat the oven to 350°F.

Combine the tamarind sauce, salt, black pepper, garlic powder, and paprika. Brush the chicken with the tamarind mixture. Brush a baking sheet with 1 teaspoon of the oil. Place the chicken on the tray. Cover with foil and bake for 1 hour.

Heat the remaining 1 teaspoon of the oil in a skillet over high heat and add the onions. Reduce heat to low. Add the raisins and almonds to the onions. Stir for 1 minute, and remove from heat. Remove the chicken from the oven and top it with the onion mixture.

———————

"*Aldik alphasich min baythitu yisich*" ("An aggressive rooster yells when he is still in the shell") expresses the idea that misbehavior is genetically derived.

Meatballs with Potatoes

كؤفتة أبيطاًطاً

Kfta ab Pateta

This hearty meal is suitable for the busy individual. Served on a bed of rice, it is filling and nourishing.

2 pounds lean ground beef, chicken, or turkey	1 medium-size onion, chopped
1 teaspoon salt	1 (4-ounce) can tomato sauce
½ teaspoon garlic powder	2 stalks celery, sliced
½ teaspoon curry powder	Juice of 1 large lemon
½ teaspoon black pepper	1 tablespoon chicken bouillon powder
½ teaspoon paprika	4 large potatoes, peeled and cubed
½ teaspoon red pepper flakes	½ cup (about 6 small) sliced button
2 teaspoons vegetable oil	mushrooms

In a bowl combine the meat, ½ teaspoon of the salt, garlic powder, curry, black pepper, paprika, and red pepper, and refrigerate for 1 hour.

Heat the vegetable oil in a pot over high heat and add the onion. Reduce heat to medium, and add 2 cups of water, the tomato sauce, celery, the remaining ½ teaspoon of salt, lemon juice, and chicken bouillon, and bring to a boil. Add the potatoes and cook until semitender (about 15 minutes).

Meanwhile, remove the meat from the refrigerator. With wet hands, form it into thirty balls. Add these meatballs to the potato mixture. Reduce heat to low, cover, and simmer for 10 minutes. Stir in the mushrooms and simmer for an additional 10 minutes.

"Mate al dik oo einu bel nachlah" ("A rooster is dying but still staring at the tree") characterizes an individual who is obsessed by greed.

Meatballs with Zucchini

كؤفتة أبقرع
Kfta ab Kara

10 SERVINGS

Serve this dish on a bed of rice, or with fresh bread and pickles. Be careful not to overcook the zucchini. If prepared properly and seasoned well, it becomes an important part of the sauce for the meatballs. The mango powder in this recipe adds flavor to the meal. It is made from raw, green mangoes that are cut, sun-dried, and pounded into powder. It can be found in Indian food stores.

½ teaspoon salt	1 medium-size onion, chopped
½ teaspoon garlic powder	1 (4-ounce) can tomato sauce
½ teaspoon black pepper	2 stalks celery, sliced
½ teaspoon red pepper flakes	4 large zucchini, cleaned and sliced
½ teaspoon mango powder	½ cup (about 6 small) sliced button
½ teaspoon paprika	mushrooms
1 teaspoon curry powder	Juice of 1 large lemon
2 pounds lean ground beef or chicken	4 large tomatoes, minced
breast	¼ cup chives, chopped
2 teaspoons olive oil	

Combine the salt, garlic powder, black pepper, red pepper, mango powder, paprika, and curry in a small bowl. Put the meat in a large bowl and into it, stir in half of the spices. Refrigerate for 1 hour.

Heat the olive oil in a pot over high heat and add the onion. Reduce heat to medium. Add 2 cups of water, the tomato sauce, celery, and the remaining spices, and bring to a boil.

Remove the meat from the refrigerator. With wet hands, form it into thirty balls. Add the meatballs to the tomato sauce. Cover and cook until the meat is tender (about 10 minutes). Then reduce heat to low, add the zucchini, and cook for 5 minutes.

Add the mushrooms, lemon juice, and tomatoes. Cover and simmer for 10 minutes. Remove from heat. Stir in the chives, and serve hot.

Meat Dishes

93

Meatballs with Pumpkin

كؤفتة أبقرع أحمر

Kfta ab Kara Hamra

My American friends were surprised to hear that I can make savory dishes with pumpkins. "Pumpkins are for pies and Halloween," they said, but when they tasted this dish, they all wanted the recipe.

½ teaspoon salt	1 (4-ounce) can tomato sauce
½ teaspoon garlic powder	1 ½ pounds pumpkin, peeled and cubed
½ teaspoon black pepper	2 stalks celery, sliced
½ teaspoon ground ginger	1 cup (about 12 small) sliced button
½ teaspoon paprika	mushrooms
½ teaspoon red pepper flakes	⅔ cup raisins
1 teaspoon curry powder	½ cup almonds
½ teaspoon cumin	3 tablespoons honey
2 pounds lean ground beef, chicken, or	1 cup sliced, dried apple
turkey	2 large tomatoes, minced
1 medium-size onion, chopped	Juice of 1 large lemon
2 teaspoons vegetable oil	

Combine the salt, garlic powder, black pepper, ginger, paprika, red pepper, curry, and cumin in a small bowl. Put the meat in a large bowl, mix with half the spices, and refrigerate covered for 1 hour.

Heat the vegetable oil in a pot over high heat and add the onion. Reduce heat to medium. Add 3 cups of water, the tomato sauce, pumpkin cubes, celery, and the remaining spices, bring to a boil, and cook until the pumpkin is semitender (about 10 minutes). Remove the meat from refrigerator and, with wet hands, form it into thirty balls. Add the meatballs to the pumpkin mixture. Stir gently and cook until the meat is tender (about 10 minutes). Reduce heat to low, and stir in the mushrooms, raisins, almonds, honey, dried apple, tomatoes, and lemon juice. Cover and simmer for 10 minutes.

A Day of Holocaust

*I*n the 1930s and '40s, the Iraqi hatred toward Jews was stoked by the Nazi movement. It reached its climax in June 1941, when with tacit government approval pogroms took place throughout the country. That day was called *El Farhud*, which meant "to rob, take possessions, destroy property, and slaughter people."

In Basra, my birthplace, the mob moved from one street to another, from one house to the next, shouting *"Mal el Yehud halal"* ("The taking of Jewish possessions is permitted by God"), leaving nothing behind. Death was everywhere. When they came to our street and wanted to enter our home, a sheikh, our neighbor, stood on our roof and fired his revolver. The mob was stunned and quieted for a brief moment, long enough for them to hear the sheikh shouting: "If you enter this home, you will have to pass through me." Fearing the authority of the sheikh, the Iraqis did not dare disobey him and spared my parents' home. Thus the devotion of a friend saved my family, as well as many other people who were hidden in our home; because the sheikh considered my father a friend, he was ready to defend him with his life.

The events of this day left the Jews of Iraq with a strong fear and a hidden desire to escape to a safe place. That day finally came in 1950 when almost all the Iraqi-Jews surrendered their possessions and accepted an "exile" to freedom in Israel.

Dumplings

كبة

Kba

Dumplings are made from a variety of doughs:

potato, semolina, bulgur, rice;

and stuffings: meat, turkey, chicken,

fish, pine nuts, almonds, raisins.

Traditionally, dumplings are special dishes

for celebrations and holidays.

Semolina Dumplings with Okra Sauce

كبة بأمية

Kba Bamia

Traditionally a cook is measured by how she prepares kba. My sister-in-law Daisy shapes the kba like an artist. Her kba are small, round, and equal in size, with very thin dough, and can be eaten in one bite. Daisy is a master of kba making.

DOUGH:
1 cup semolina
1 teaspoon salt
1 teaspoon ground turmeric
1 cup boiling water
½ cup all-purpose flour

STUFFING:
2 teaspoons vegetable oil
1 medium-size onion, chopped
2 pounds lean ground beef, chicken, or turkey
½ teaspoon salt
½ teaspoon garlic powder
½ teaspoon black pepper

½ cup chopped fresh parsley

OKRA SAUCE:
2 teaspoons vegetable oil
1 medium-size onion, chopped
2 pounds fresh okra, chopped
1 (8-ounce) can tomato sauce
½ teaspoon salt
½ teaspoon black pepper
½ teaspoon paprika
½ teaspoon celery seed
Juice of 1 large lemon
2 tablespoons honey
4 large tomatoes, minced

Combine the semolina, salt, and turmeric in a large bowl. Pour in the boiling water, mix, and cool. Add the flour, and mix in to firm the dough. Cover and set aside.

Heat the vegetable oil in a large pot over high heat and add the onion. Reduce heat to medium. Add the meat,

CONTINUED

salt, garlic powder, and black pepper, and cook until the meat is tender (about 10 minutes). Remove from heat, stir in the parsley, and cool.

Divide the dough into thirty pieces. Put 1 cup of cold water in a bowl. Use this water to wet your hands before shaping each kba so that the dough will not stick to your hands. Flatten each piece of dough in your palm. Put 2 tablespoons of the stuffing in the center of each piece of the dough. Fold the dough over to cover the stuffing, then pinch the edges of the dough to seal it in. Roll each kba in your hands to make a ball, flatten it slightly, and set aside.

SAUCE:

Heat the vegetable oil in a large pot over high heat and add the onion. Reduce heat to medium, and add the okra, tomato sauce, and 2 cups of water, and bring to a boil. Stir in the salt, black pepper, paprika, and celery seed, and cook until the okra is tender (about 20 minutes). Reduce heat to low, add the lemon juice and the honey, cover and simmer until the dough is tender (about 10 minutes). Stir in the tomatoes. Add the dumplings to the sauce, one at a time, stirring gently so that they do not stick to the bottom of the pot. Simmer until the dough is tender (about 10 minutes).

Meat and Raisin Bulgur Dumplings

كبة برغل ؤقشمش

Kba Bulgur ab Kishmish

This kba is filled with raisins and meat. It is served on holidays, at weddings, and for other celebrations. I fondly remember my mother visiting us in the United States. We loved this kba so much that she prepared it for us at least once a week. My brother Oved and his children could not wait until all the kba were made, and are stood beside her while she fried the kba, eating them as soon as they were removed from the skillet. It takes time to make this kba, but it is worth the effort.

DOUGH:	1 pound chicken or beef, finely chopped
1 cup bulgur	½ teaspoon salt
½ teaspoon salt	½ teaspoon garlic powder
½ teaspoon ground cumin	½ teaspoon black pepper
2 cups boiling water	½ teaspoon red pepper flakes
½ cup all-purpose flour	¼ teaspoon ground nutmeg
	1 teaspoon curry powder
STUFFING:	⅔ cup raisins
2 tablespoons vegetable oil	½ cup pine nuts
1 medium-size onion, chopped	½ teaspoon ground turmeric

Combine the bulgur, salt, and cumin in a large bowl. Add the boiling water and mix to form a dough. Cover and set aside for 15 minutes. Then add the flour and mix into a firm dough. Set aside for an additional 15 minutes.

Heat the vegetable oil in a large pan over high heat and add the onion. Reduce heat to medium. Add the meat and stir until it is tender (about 10 minutes). Stir in the salt, garlic powder, black pepper, red pepper, nutmeg, and curry. Reduce heat to low. Add the raisins and pine nuts, and simmer for 2 minutes. Set aside to cool.

CONTINUED

Dumplings

Divide the dough into ten pieces.

Put 1 cup of water in a bowl. Use the water to wet your hands before shaping each kba so that the dough does not stick to them. Flatten each piece of dough in your palm. Put 2 tablespoons of the stuffing in the center of each piece of the dough. Fold over the dough to cover the stuffing, then pinch the edges of the dough to seal it in. Roll each kba in your hands to make a ball, and flatten it slightly.

Bring 4 cups of water and the turmeric to a boil in a pot. Reduce heat to medium. Put a few kba at a time into the boiling water. Stir gently so that they do not stick to the bottom. Cook for 3 minutes, remove from water and set aside to dry. Heat the vegetable oil in a pan over medium heat. Reduce heat to low and fry each kba until golden brown on both sides.

Semolina Dumplings with Zucchini

كبة حمؤصطة

Kba Hamusta

My mother taught me to use the side of a wooden spoon to break up the meat as you are cooking it. This makes a smooth stuffing for each kba.

DOUGH:

2 cups semolina

1 teaspoon salt

1 teaspoon ground turmeric

2 cups boiling water

1 cup all-purpose flour

STUFFING:

2 teaspoons vegetable oil

1 medium-size onion, chopped

1½ pounds lean ground beef

½ cup chopped fresh parsley

½ teaspoon salt

½ teaspoon garlic powder

½ teaspoon black pepper

½ teaspoon red pepper flakes

½ teaspoon ground cumin

SAUCE:

2 teaspoons vegetable oil

1 medium-size onion, chopped

1 (4-ounce) can tomato sauce

½ teaspoon salt

½ teaspoon garlic powder

1 teaspoon curry powder

½ teaspoon ground ginger

2 large zucchini, cleaned and sliced

½ pound spinach, stemmed and chopped

Juice of 2 large lemons

Combine the semolina, salt, and turmeric in a large bowl. Stir in the boiling water and cool. Mix in the flour, cover, and set aside.

Heat the vegetable oil in a large pan over high heat and add the onion. Add the meat and stir for 2 minutes. Reduce heat to medium. Stir in the parsley, salt, garlic powder, black pepper, red pepper, and cumin. Reduce heat to low. Simmer until the meat is tender (about 10 minutes), and set aside to cool.

CONTINUED

Divide the dough into forty pieces. Put 1 cup of cold water in a bowl. Use this water to wet your hands before preparing each kba so that the dough does not stick to them. Flatten each piece of dough in your palm. Put 2 tablespoons of the stuffing in the center of each piece of the dough. Fold the dough over to cover the stuffing, then pinch the edges of the dough to seal it in. Roll each kba in your hands to make a ball, flatten it slightly, and set aside.

SAUCE:

Heat the vegetable oil over high heat in a large pot and add the onion. Add 2½ cups of water, the tomato sauce, salt, garlic powder, curry, and ginger, and bring to a boil. Reduce heat to medium. Stir in the zucchini and spinach. Add the kba one at a time and stir gently so that the dumplings do not stick to the bottom of the pot. Reduce heat to low. Add the lemon juice and stir gently so you do not break the kba. Cover and simmer until the semolina dough is tender (for about 15 minutes).

Dumplings with Rice, Meat, and Pine Nuts

كبة حلأب

Kba Halab

If you have leftover stuffing, it may be mixed with an egg, shaped into patties, and fried.

DOUGH:	½ teaspoon salt
4 cups cooked rice	½ teaspoon garlic powder
1 cup all-purpose flour	½ teaspoon paprika
½ teaspoon salt	½ teaspoon red pepper flakes
½ teaspoon ground cumin	1 teaspoon curry powder
	Juice of 1 large lemon
STUFFING:	4 teaspoons olive oil
2 pounds lean beef, chicken breast, or	2 medium-size onions, chopped
turkey, finely chopped	2 tablespoons pine nuts

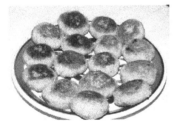

Combine the rice, flour, salt, and cumin in a large bowl. Add 1 cup of water and mix to make a dough. Cover and set aside.

Next, combine the meat, salt, garlic powder, paprika, red pepper, curry, and lemon juice in a large bowl, cover, and refrigerate for ½ hour.

Heat 2 teaspoons of the olive oil in a pot over high heat and add the onions. Reduce heat to medium. Stir in the meat, and cook until it is tender (about 10 minutes). Reduce heat to low. Add the pine nuts, and stir for 1 minute. Remove from heat and cool.

Divide the dough into twenty pieces. Put 1 cup of cold water in a bowl. Use this water to wet your hands before shaping each kba so that the dough will not stick to your hands.

CONTINUED

Flatten each piece of dough in your palm. Put 2 tablespoons of the stuffing in the center of each piece of the dough. Fold the dough over to cover the stuffing, then pinch the edges of the dough to seal it in.

Roll each kba in your hands to make a ball, and flatten it slightly.

Brush a skillet over low heat with the remaining olive oil. Fry the kba until golden brown on both sides.

Meat and Potato Dumplings

عرؤق بطأطأ ؤلحم

Aurook Pateta oo Lahm

Meat and potato dumplings are a Jewish Iraqi specialty. They are made for all holidays, especially Hanukkah, the celebration of freedom. They are served hot or cold as a main dish, or as a snack.

DOUGH:	½ teaspoon hot paprika
8 large potatoes, peeled and chopped	½ teaspoon ginger ground
½ teaspoon salt	1 teaspoon curry powder
	Juice of 1 large lemon
STUFFING:	4 tablespoons vegetable oil
2 pounds lean ground lean beef, chicken, or turkey	2 medium-size onions, chopped
	⅔ cup raisins
½ teaspoon salt	1 egg, lightly beaten
½ teaspoon garlic powder	

Put 3 cups of water, the potatoes, and salt in a large pot, and bring to a boil. Reduce heat to medium. Cook until the potatoes are tender (about 10 minutes) and mash.

Combine the meat, salt, garlic powder, paprika, ginger, curry, and lemon juice in a separate bowl, cover, and refrigerate for ½ hour.

Heat 1 tablespoon of the vegetable oil in a pan over high heat and add the onions. Reduce heat to medium. Stir in the meat mixture and cook until it is tender (about 10 minutes). Reduce heat to low. Add the raisins, mix, and cook for 2 minutes, stirring. Remove from heat and cool.

CONTINUED

Dumplings

Divide the mashed potatoes into twenty pieces. Put 1 cup of cold water in a bowl. Use this water to wet your hands before shaping each kba so that the dough will not stick to it.

Flatten each portion of potatoes in your palm. Put 2 tablespoons of the stuffing in the center of each piece. Fold the potatoes over to cover the stuffing, then pinch the edges of the dough to seal it in. Roll each kba in your hands to make a ball, and flatten it slightly.

Brush the dumplings with egg. Heat the remaining vegetable oil in a pan. Reduce heat to low. Fry each kba until golden brown on both sides.

Fish, Rice, and Semolina Dumplings

كبة أبسمك

Kba ab Samak

This dish requires a rather lengthy preparation. Some make the dough without semolina and add white flour instead. My sister-in-law Daisy omits both the flour and the semolina; she makes the shell of the kba entirely from cooked rice and adds a beaten egg to firm up the dough. I found that semolina and rice dough gives more flavor.

DOUGH:

½ cup semolina

½ teaspoon salt

½ teaspoon black pepper

½ teaspoon ground cumin

2 teaspoons dried dill

1 cup boiling water

2 cups cooked rice

STUFFING:

2 pounds fish fillets such as cod, sole, trout, or red snapper

4 tablespoons vegetable oil

1 medium-size onion, chopped

¼ cup chopped fresh cilantro

¼ cup chopped chives

¼ cup chopped fresh parsley

½ teaspoon salt

½ teaspoon ground turmeric

½ teaspoon white pepper

½ teaspoon garlic powder

½ teaspoon red pepper flakes

Juice of 1 large lemon

Combine the semolina, salt, black pepper, cumin, and dill in a large bowl. Stir in the boiling water and set aside for 10 minutes. Add the cooked rice and mix to form the dough.

Put 2 cups of water in a pot and bring to a boil, then reduce heat to medium. Place the fish in a strainer, and suspend the strainer over the boiling water. Cover the strainer with the pot lid and steam the fish until it is tender (about 10 minutes). Mash and set aside.

CONTINUED

Heat 1 tablespoon of the vegetable oil over high heat and add the onion. Reduce heat to medium. Stir in the cilantro, chives, parsley, salt, turmeric, white pepper, garlic powder, and red pepper. Add the fish and lemon juice, mix, and cook for an additional 2 minutes. Remove from heat and cool.

Divide the dough into twenty pieces.

Put 1 cup of water in a bowl. Use the water to wet your hands before forming each *kba* so that the dough will not stick to them. Flatten each piece of dough in your palm.

Put 2 tablespoons of the stuffing in the center of each piece of dough. Fold the dough over to cover the stuffing. Then pinch the edges of the dough to seal it in. Roll each kba in your hands to make a ball, and flatten it slightly.

Heat the remaining 3 tablespoons of oil. Reduce heat to low, and fry the kba until golden brown on both sides.

Stuffed Vegetables and Stuffed Meat

محشة

M'hasha

Stuffed meats are usually prepared for holidays and other special occasions though they are sometimes served as part of a regular meal. Traditionally we make ample use of what the environment offers. Since vegetables are abundant all year round, they are always available to make up these popular dishes. Vegetables such as turnips, zucchini, green leaves, and grape leaves, stuffed with rice, and meat, turkey, or chicken, blended with a variety of spices, can be served hot or cold.

Zucchini Stuffed with Meat

محشة أبقرع وَلحم

M'hasha Karh oo Lahm

M'hasha is a Jewish -Arabic word meaning "to stuff." Almost any vegetable can be stuffed with meat and rice, and stuffed zucchini in particular makes a great meal, served hot or cold and with pickles.

---

8 large zucchini, cut crosswise into thirds

STUFFING:

1 pound lean ground beef, chicken, or turkey

½ teaspoon salt

½ teaspoon garlic powder

¼ teaspoon ground nutmeg

½ teaspoon hot paprika

¼ teaspoon ground cinnamon

½ teaspoon ground ginger

2 teaspoons vegetable oil

1 medium-size onion, chopped

1 stalk celery, chopped

¼ cup chopped fresh cilantro

½ cup (about 6 small) chopped button mushrooms

1 cup cooked rice

SAUCE:

1 (8-ounce) can tomato sauce

Juice of 1 large lemon

½ teaspoon salt

½ teaspoon garlic powder

¼ teaspoon black pepper

Scoop out the interior of each zucchini to form a hollow cylinder. Then chop up the interiors and set aside.

Combine the meat, salt, garlic powder, nutmeg, paprika, cinnamon, and ginger in a bowl, and refrigerate for ½ hour.

Heat the vegetable oil in a pot over high heat and add the onion. Reduce heat to medium, add the meat to the onion, and stir for 2 minutes. Add the chopped zucchini , celery, and cilantro, and cook until the meat is tender (about 10 minutes). Reduce heat to low. Stir in the mushrooms and rice. Cover and simmer for 5 minutes. Remove from heat.

CONTINUED

Stuffed Vegetables and Stuffed Meat

Preheat oven to 400°F.

Fill the zucchini cylinders with the stuffing and place on baking sheet.

Combine the tomato sauce, 1 cup of water, lemon juice, salt, garlic powder, and black pepper in a bowl. Pour the sauce over the stuffed zucchini. Cover with aluminum foil and bake for ½ hour. Serve hot.

"*El fat mat*" ("The past is dead") refers to the idea that a person should focus on the positive present and future rather than the negative past.

Green Leaves Stuffed with Meat

محشة أبسلق ؤلحم
M'hasha ab Selk

This dish is served at family gatherings. You will need a lot of time and a large working area to prepare it. The end result is a fabulous dish whose aroma lasts through the entire meal.

---

40 fresh large green leaves (beets, Swiss chard, or collards)

STUFFING:
2 pounds lean ground beef, chicken, or turkey
½ teaspoon salt
½ teaspoon garlic powder
½ teaspoon curry powder
½ teaspoon hot paprika
½ teaspoon dried thyme
½ teaspoon ground ginger
2 teaspoons olive oil
2 medium-size onions, chopped
1 stalk celery, chopped
¼ cup chopped fresh parsley

½ cup (about 6 small) chopped button mushrooms
1 cup cooked rice
Juice of 1 large lemon

SAUCE:
1 (8-ounce) can tomato sauce
Juice of 1 large lemon
2 tablespoons honey
½ teaspoon salt
½ teaspoon hot paprika
½ teaspoon garlic powder
½ teaspoon dried oregano
1 tablespoon chopped fresh mint

In a large pot bring 3 cups of water to a boil. Dip a few leaves at a time into the boiling water for 1 minute. This will soften the leaves and make them pliable. Remove the leaves from the boiling water and place them on a tray.

Combine the meat, salt, garlic powder, curry, paprika, thyme, and ginger in a bowl, and refrigerate for ½ hour.

Heat the olive oil in a pan over high heat and add the onions. Reduce heat to medium. Stir in the meat, celery, and parsley, and cook until the meat is tender (about 10 minutes).

CONTINUED

Reduce heat to low, and add the mushrooms, rice, and lemon juice. Cover and simmer for 2 minutes. Remove from heat and cool.

Put each leaf on a flat surface. Place 2 tablespoons of stuffing in the center of each leaf. Fold the edges in and roll up the long way. Put the stuffed leaves on a baking sheet and set aside.

Preheat oven to 400°F.

SAUCE:

In a small pot, combine the tomato sauce, lemon juice, honey, salt, paprika, garlic powder, oregano, and 2 cups of water, and bring to a boil. Stir in the mint.

Pour the sauce over stuffed leaves, cover with aluminum foil, and bake for ½ hour.

Grape Leaves Stuffed with Meat

يبرأح

Yaprach

Yaprach are mainly prepared by Jews who lived where grapes are grown, in northern Iraq or in Kurdistan.

---

40 large grape leaves from a jar, stemmed, or, fresh grape leaves boiled for 5 minutes and stemmed

STUFFING:
1 pound lean ground beef or chicken
½ teaspoon salt
½ teaspoon garlic powder
½ teaspoon hot paprika
½ teaspoon black pepper
½ teaspoon ground cinnamon
¼ teaspoon ground nutmeg
2 teaspoons olive oil

1 medium-size onion, chopped
1 stalk celery, chopped
1 cup cooked rice
1 large tomato, chopped
¼ cup chopped fresh mint

SAUCE:
¼ cup chopped fresh parsley
½ teaspoon salt
½ teaspoon black pepper
Juice of 1 large lemon
2 teaspoons olive oil

Combine the meat, salt, garlic powder, paprika, black pepper, cinnamon, and nutmeg in a bowl, and refrigerate for ½ hour.

Preheat the oven to 400°F.

Heat the olive oil in a pan over high heat and add the onion. Reduce heat to medium, add the meat, and stir for 2 minutes. Add the celery and cook until the meat is tender (about 10 minutes). Reduce heat to low. Stir in the rice, tomato, and mint, and simmer for 2 minutes. Remove from heat and cool.

CONTINUED

Place each grape leaf on a flat surface. Put 2 tablespoons of stuffing in the center of each leaf, fold the edges in and roll up the long way. Arrange the stuffed leaves neatly on a baking sheet.

SAUCE:
Combine the parsley, salt, black pepper, lemon juice, and olive oil in a bowl. Add 2 cups of water, and bring to a boil.

Pour the sauce over the stuffed leaves, cover with aluminum foil and bake for 45 minutes.

———————————

"Einu juana oo batnoo shibanah" ("His eyes are hungry, but his stomach is full.") describes a person who desires food even though he is not hungry; he will not share it with others.

Quince Stuffed with Meat

محشة أبحؤه وؤلحم

M'hasha ab Hawa

Quinces are fabulous fruits. They look like pears and smell like pineapple. They are used in a variety of ways: prepared as a main dish stuffed with meat, boiled in water and served hot with honey on a cold day. My aunt Habiba loves quinces. She makes them sweet by adding two tablespoons of honey to the stuffing. The honey and spices blend well with the meat.

1 pound lean ground beef or chicken	**STUFFING:**
½ teaspoon salt	2 teaspoons vegetable oil
½ teaspoon garlic powder	
½ teaspoon hot paprika	1 medium-size onion, chopped
½ teaspoon ground cumin	1 tablespoon pine nuts
¼ teaspoon ground nutmeg	⅓ cup raisins
¼ teaspoon ground cinnamon	Juice of 1 large lemon
¼ teaspoon ground ginger	
4 quinces, halved	**SAUCE:**
	½ cup sweet red wine, such as Concord grape
	Juice of 1 large lemon
	2 tablespoons of honey
	½ teaspoon ground cinnamon

Scoop out the interior of each quince to form a pocket. Chop up the interiors and set aside.

Combine the meat, salt, garlic powder, paprika, cumin, nutmeg, cinnamon, and ginger in a bowl, and refrigerate for ½ hour.

Heat the vegetable oil in a pan over high heat and add the onion. Reduce heat to medium. Add the meat and chopped quince, and stir for 2 minutes. Cover and cook until the meat is tender (about 10 minutes). Reduce heat to low. Add the

CONTINUED

pine nuts, raisins, and lemon juice, and simmer for 2 minutes. Remove from heat. Fill each quince half with the meat mixture, and place neatly on a baking sheet.

Preheat oven to 375°F.

SAUCE:

Combine the wine, lemon juice, honey, cinnamon, and 1 cup of water in a bowl.

Pour the sauce over the stuffed quinces. Cover with aluminum foil and bake for 1 hour.

Chicken Stuffed with Meat

تبيت

Tebit

10 SERVINGS

No Jewish Iraqi Sabbath table is complete without tebit. Because the cooking cannot be done on Saturday, tebit is prepared on Friday and cooked overnight, to be served the following day. My sister Aya puts a peeled hard-boiled egg in the center of the stuffing; when the tebit is sliced, the egg creates a pleasant presentation.

1 (3-pound) chicken, skin removed	1 cup cooked rice
	1 large tomato, chopped
STUFFING	
½ teaspoon salt	**SAUCE:**
¼ teaspoon ground cardamom	2 teaspoons vegetable oil
¼ teaspoon ground nutmeg	1 small onion, chopped
¼ teaspoon ground cinnamon	1 (8-ounce) can tomato sauce
¼ teaspoon black pepper	½ teaspoon salt
¼ teaspoon white pepper	½ teaspoon garlic powder
¼ teaspoon hot paprika	Juice of 1 large lemon
2 teaspoons vegetable oil	1½ cups rice
1 small onion, chopped	
½ pound lean ground beef or ground chicken breast	

Preheat the oven to 200°F.

Combine the salt, cardamom, nutmeg, cinnamon, black pepper, white pepper, and paprika in a bowl.

Heat the vegetable oil in a pan over high heat and add the onion. Reduce heat to medium. Stir in the meat and half the spices, and cook for 5 minutes. Stir in the rice and tomato, for 1 minute, and remove from heat.

CONTINUED

Stuffed Vegetables and Stuffed Meat   121

Stuff the chicken with the meat mixture. Sprinkle the remaining half the spices over the chicken, and place the stuffed chicken in a roasting pan.

SAUCE:

Heat the vegetable oil in a pot over high heat and add the onion. Reduce heat to medium and stir in the tomato sauce and 4 cups of water. Add the salt, garlic powder, lemon juice, and rice, and remove from heat.

Pour the rice mixture around the chicken. Cover with aluminum foil and bake for 8 hours or overnight at 200°F.

> # Jewish Iraqi cuisine traveled with me from Iraq to Jerusalem to the United States.
>
> I do not have any pictures from my life in Iraq, since we were not allowed to take anything with us when we left except the clothing we had on. However the pilot stove in the picture above is a memento of the beginning of our life in Israel. On it we cooked our meals and maintained our Jewish Iraqi cuisine, and heated water for washing, cleaning, and laundry. The stove traveled with me to the United States. Today it stands in my home, settled by my fireplace in

Stuffed Meat Pockets

حشؤه أبلحم

Hashwa ab Lahm

For this dish, long-grain, white rice is preferable to give it a fluffy texture. Traditionally, the stuffing for this meal is made of rice and meat but vegetables are my mother's contribution.

---

3 pounds beef shoulder, sliced ¼ inch
  thick
½ teaspoon salt
½ teaspoon garlic powder
½ teaspoon ground ginger
½ teaspoon ground cumin
½ teaspoon curry powder
¼ teaspoon ground coriander

STUFFING:
2 teaspoons vegetable oil
1 medium-size onion, chopped
½ pound chicken breast, chopped
½ teaspoon salt
½ teaspoon garlic powder
¼ teaspoon ground cinnamon
¼ teaspoon ground cardamom
½ teaspoon ground ginger
½ teaspoon black pepper

½ teaspoon hot paprika
1 large zucchini, chopped
¼ cup chopped fresh cilantro
½ cup (about 6 small) chopped button
  mushrooms
1 cup cooked rice
a needle and white thread

SAUCE:
2 teaspoons vegetable oil
1 small onion, chopped
½ teaspoon salt
½ teaspoon garlic powder
½ teaspoon hot paprika
¼ teaspoon dried thyme
1 (8-ounce) can tomato sauce
¼ cup chopped fresh parsley
2 large tomatoes, chopped

In a bowl combine the beef, salt, garlic powder, ginger, cumin, curry, and coriander. Refrigerate for ½ hour.

Heat the vegetable oil in a pan over high heat and add the onion. Reduce heat to medium. Add the chicken, salt, garlic powder, cinnamon, cardamom, ginger, black pepper, and paprika, and cook for 2 minutes, stirring. Stir in the zucchini and cilantro, and cook for 2 minutes. Remove from heat. Add the mushrooms and rice, and set aside to cool.

CONTINUED

Stuffed Vegetables and Stuffed Meat

Place one slice of meat on the top of a second slice and sew 3 of the sides together with a needle and thread to form a pocket.

Fill each pocket with the chicken mixture and sew the fourth side shut to seal in the stuffing. Place the stuffed beef in a roasting pan.

Preheat the oven to 400°F.

Heat the vegetable oil in a pan over high heat and add the onion. Reduce heat to medium. Stir in the salt, garlic powder, paprika, and thyme. Add 1½ cups of water and the tomato sauce, and bring to a boil. Remove from heat and add the parsley and tomatoes. Pour the sauce over the stuffed meat. Cover with aluminum foil and bake for 1½ hours.

Fish

דגים سمك

Samak

The Shaat al Arab is the confluence of the Tigris
and Euphrates Rivers. According to the Bible,
these rivers ran through the Garden of Eden and
many varieties of fish are abundant in them.
Iraqi Jews made use of the offerings of their
environment by creating numerous fish dishes.

Garlic and Basil Fish

سمك أبثؤم ؤغيحأن
Samak ab Thum oo Rihan

Fish has magical and mystic properties. We use the head of a fish in our New Year's celebration in the hope that we will always be at the head of things, so to speak, and not falling behind.

2 teaspoons olive oil	½ teaspoon paprika
1 large onion, sliced	½ teaspoon red pepper flakes
4 large tomatoes, minced	Juice of 2 large lemons
10 garlic cloves, sliced	3 pounds fish fillets such as cod, sole,
½ teaspoon salt	trout, or red snapper, cleaned and
½ teaspoon black pepper	chopped
½ teaspoon ground cumin	1 cup chopped fresh basil

Heat the olive oil in a large pan over high heat and add the onion. Reduce heat to medium. Stir in the tomatoes, garlic, salt, black pepper, cumin, paprika, red pepper, lemon juice, and 1 cup of water. Bring to a boil, then reduce heat to low and simmer for 5 minutes. Add the fish and basil. Stir gently and simmer until the fish is fully cooked (about 15 minutes).

"Aind alla amah b'aidi" ("It is not far from God's reach") means to keep on believing, keep on hoping, never give up; miracles can happen. This metaphor is used on a daily basis.

Fish Patties

عرؤق أبسمك

Aurook ab Samak

This dish is an excellent use of leftover fish. Almost any kind of fish can be prepared the same way as in this recipe.

2 pounds fish fillets such as cod, sole, trout, or red snapper, cooked and flaked	½ teaspoon salt
	½ teaspoon black pepper
	½ teaspoon curry powder
1 cup cooked rice	½ teaspoon paprika
½ cup (about 4) chopped scallions	½ teaspoon red pepper flakes (optional)
¼ cup chopped fresh cilantro	Juice of 1 large lemon
2 stalks celery, chopped	3 eggs, lightly beaten
1 large tomato, chopped	2 tablespoons vegetable oil
4 cloves garlic, minced	

Combine the fish, rice, scallions, cilantro, celery, tomato, garlic, salt, black pepper, curry, paprika, red pepper, and lemon juice in a bowl, then mix in the eggs.

Heat the vegetable oil in a pan over high heat and reduce heat to low. Drop in tablespoons of the mixture and fry until golden brown on both sides.
Transfer to a paper towel to soak up the oil. Place the fish patties on a platter and serve hot or cold.

Fish in Tomato-Garlic Sauce

صألؤنأ
Salona

Salona is prepared mostly in the winter, served hot on a bed of rice. This moist fish in a garlic and tomato sauce goes especially well with sweet and spicy condiments. You can make this dish from fresh or leftover fish.

2 pounds fish fillets such as cod, sole, trout, or red snapper, cleaned and cut into large pieces	*½ teaspoon ground turmeric*
	½ teaspoon black pepper
	½ teaspoon paprika
2 tablespoons fresh lemon juice	*¼ teaspoon ground cumin*
2 teaspoons vegetable oil	
3 medium-size onions, sliced	*2 tablespoons white wine vinegar*
1 (4-ounce) can tomato sauce	*2 tablespoons honey or sugar*
½ cup green chile peppers, chopped	*3 large tomatoes, sliced*
8 cloves garlic, sliced	*¼ cup chopped fresh parsley*
½ teaspoon salt	

Combine the fish with the lemon juice in a bowl. Marinate in the refrigerator for 15 minutes. Put 2 cups of water in a pot and bring to a boil, then reduce heat to medium. Place the fish in a strainer, and suspend the strainer over the boiling water. Cover the strainer with the pot lid and steam until fish is tender (about 10 minutes). Remove from heat and set aside.

Heat the vegetable oil in a pot over high heat and add the onion. Add 1 cup of water and the tomato sauce. Reduce heat to medium. Stir in the chile peppers, garlic powder, salt, turmeric, black pepper, paprika, and cumin, and bring to a boil.

Reduce heat to low. Stir in the vinegar and honey, and simmer for 2 minutes. Arrange the fish evenly in the sauce. Put the tomato slices neatly on the top of the fish and sprinkle with parsley. Simmer for 10 minutes.

Salmon with Tamarind Sauce

سمك مشوّى أبتمر هندى

Samak M'shyee ab Tamar Hindi

Mixing tamarind sauce with lemon, herbs, spices, and serving on a bed of rice, makes a delightful meal with a lovely aroma. This dish is impressive and easy to make; tamarind sauce can be obtained from Middle Eastern shops.

3 pounds salmon (half a whole fish, filleted), cleaned	4 garlic cloves, crushed
Juice of 1 large lemon	½ cup chopped fresh cilantro
1 tablespoon olive oil	½ teaspoon salt
1 medium-size onion, chopped	½ teaspoon black pepper
	½ cup tamarind sauce

Marinate the fish in the lemon juice and refrigerate for ½ an hour. Brush a baking sheet with 1 teaspoon of the olive oil. Place the fish on the baking sheet.

Preheat oven to 450°F.

Heat the the remaining olive oil in a pan over high heat and add the onion. Stir in the garlic, cilantro, salt, and black pepper. Spread the tamarind sauce evenly over the fish. Top the fish with the onion mixture and bake for ½ hour. Serve hot or cold.

———————

"Aklo ma maloo. Ruhoo ma maloo?" ("The food is not his. Is his soul not his?") refers to overeating and poor food choices, which hinder body and soul.

Trout with Lemon and Garlic

سمك حأمض وؤثؤم
Samak Hamuth oo Thum

One of the best ways of cooking fish is baking it in the oven. Alternately it can be broiled. But trout is especially tasty when stuffed with lemon and onion.

1 large onion, chopped	*½ teaspoon black pepper*
4 cloves garlic, crushed	*½ teaspoon red pepper flakes*
Juice of 1 large lemon	*1 (3-pound) trout, eviscerated and*
½ teaspoon salt	*cleaned*

Combine the onion, garlic, lemon juice, salt, black pepper, and red pepper in a bowl and set aside. Place the fish on even surface. With a sharp knife cut through the fish bone to enlarge the opening to the interior to make a larger pouch. Rinse the fish again, then stuff the interior with the onion mixture, and refrigerate for 2 hours.

Preheat the oven to 450°F.

Remove the fish from the refrigerator and place it on a baking sheet. Cover with aluminum foil and bake for 20 minutes. Serve hot on a bed of rice.

Fish with Tomato-Lemon Sauce

محّوّه
M'hawa

8 SERVINGS

M'hawa is always served hot on a bed of rice. The alternating layers of fish, tomato, and lemon add color that enhances the presentation of the dish. The sauce for this dish is slightly acidic. Blended with the spices, it provides fragrance and flavor. The mango powder in this recipe can be found in Indian and Middle Eastern stores.

2 pounds fish fillets such as cod, sole, trout, or red snapper, cut into 8 pieces	½ teaspoon red pepper flakes (optional)
Juice of 1 large lemon	½ teaspoon curry powder
2 teaspoons vegetable oil	1 teaspoon dried dill
2 medium onions, chopped	1 teaspoon celery seeds
1 (4-ounce) can tomato sauce	1 teaspoon mango powder
4 garlic cloves, crushed	2 tablespoons sugar
½ teaspoon salt	2 large lemons, sliced with seeds removed
½ teaspoon black pepper	4 large tomatoes, sliced
	¼ cup chopped fresh parsley

Combine the fish with the lemon juice in a bowl. Refrigerate for 1 hour.

Heat the vegetable oil in a pot over high heat and add the onions. Reduce heat to medium. Add the tomato sauce, garlic, 1 cup of water, salt, black pepper, red pepper, curry, dill, celery seeds, and mango powder, stir, and bring to a boil. Reduce heat to low. Stir in the sugar and remove from heat.

Line the bottom of a second large pot with the lemon slices. Top them with a layer of fish, and then a layer of the tomato slices. Do not stir. Pour the sauce over the tomato slices. Cover the pot with its lid and simmer over low heat until the fish is tender (about 20 minutes).

Remove from heat and arrange on a platter. Sprinkle with the parsley. Serve hot or cold.

132

Mama Nazima's Jewish-Iraqi Cuisine

Baked Salmon

سمك مشوّى
Samak M'shyee

Traditionally my family serves this salmon dish with rice, pickled lemon, and various colorful steamed vegetables. The salmon is marinated with lemon and refrigerated for one hour to allow for effective absorption of the lemon.

3 pounds salmon fillet (half a whole fish)	*½ teaspoon ground ginger*
Juice of 2 large lemons	*½ teaspoon paprika*
½ teaspoon salt	*½ teaspoon red pepper flakes*
1 teaspoon dried dill	*½ teaspoon garlic powder*
½ teaspoon black pepper	

Combine the salmon with the lemon juice and refrigerate for 1 hour.

Preheat the oven to 450°F.

Combine the salt, dill, black pepper, ginger, paprika, red pepper, and garlic powder in a small bowl.

Remove the salmon from the refrigerator and place it on a baking sheet. Sprinkle the spice mixture over the salmon, cover with aluminum foil, and bake for 30 minutes. Serve hot or cold.

Fish in Eggplant Sauce

إنكرى أبسمك

Engreyee ab Samak

8 SERVINGS

This is a dish for special occasions. It is served with a mound of white rice on a large platter. Arrange the fish and vegetables over the rice, then pour the sauce over everything.

1 eggplant, peeled and sliced ¼ inch thick	1 teaspoon curry powder
1½ teaspoons salt	4 carrots, peeled and sliced
1 tablespoon vegetable oil	2 zucchini, sliced
2 pounds fish fillets such as cod, sole, trout, or red snapper, chopped	3 crookneck squash, sliced
2 medium-size onions, chopped	½ cup (about 6 small) chopped button mushrooms
1 (8-ounce) can tomato sauce	Juice of 1 large lemon
½ teaspoon red pepper flakes	1 tablespoon sugar
½ teaspoon black pepper	
¼ teaspoon ground ginger	

Sprinkle the eggplant with 1 teaspoon of the salt and set aside for 1 hour in a strainer. Then gently squeeze the eggplant slices to remove any liquid. Heat the oil in a pan over high heat. Reduce heat to medium and fry the eggplant until golden brown on both sides. Place the fried eggplant on paper towels to soak up the oil.

Put 2 cups of water in a pot and bring to a boil, then reduce heat to medium. Place the fish in a strainer, and suspend the strainer over the boiling water. Cover the strainer with the pot lid and steam the fish until it is tender (about 10 minutes). Remove from heat and set aside.

134

Mama Nazima's Jewish-Iraqi Cuisine

Preheat the oven to 350°F.

Put the onions, tomato sauce, and 1½ cups of water in a pot over high heat and bring to a boil. Reduce heat to medium.

Stir in the remaining ½ teaspoon of the salt, the red pepper, black pepper, ginger, and curry. Add the carrots and cook for 3 minutes. Add the zucchini and cook for 3 minutes. Reduce heat to low. Add the crookneck squash, and cook for 3 minutes. Add the mushrooms, lemon juice, sugar, and fried eggplant, and remove from heat.

Place the fish neatly on a baking sheet. Pour the sauce over the fish. Cover with aluminum foil and bake for 20 minutes.

Salmon with Vegetables

مزكؤفة أبقرع
Masgufa ab Kara

Masgufa is one of the most popular fish dishes. When I was a child, my mother prepared it every Thursday. There are different versions of *masgufa*: cooked with vegetables, with sauce only, or just marinated with spices and lemon crystal. Our favorite *masgufa* is made with vegetables.

3 pounds salmon (half a whole fish), cut lengthwise	½ teaspoon salt
	1 teaspoon mango powder
Juice of 1 large lemon	½ teaspoon curry powder
	½ teaspoon black pepper
VEGETABLE TOPPING:	½ teaspoon paprika
2 teaspoons olive oil	Juice of 1 large lemon
2 medium-size onions, sliced	1 teaspoon dried dill
2 stalks celery, chopped	½ cup (about 6 small) chopped button
2 large zucchini, chopped	mushrooms
2 crookneck squash, chopped	2 large tomatoes, sliced
4 cloves garlic, crushed	¼ cup chopped fresh parsley

Preheat oven to 450°F.

Marinate the fish in the juice of 1 large lemon, and refrigerate for ½ hour. Bake for 20 minutes.

VEGETABLE TOPPING:
Heat the olive oil in a pan over high heat and add the onions, and reduce heat to medium. Stir in the celery and zucchini, and cook for 2 minutes. Stir in the crookneck squash and garlic, and cook for 2 minutes. Reduce heat to low, and add the salt, mango powder, curry, black pepper, paprika, lemon juice, and dill. Add the mushrooms, and cook for 1 minute. Remove from heat and pour the mixture over the fish.

Top with the tomato slices, and sprinkle with parsley.

Bake uncovered for 10 minutes.

Fish with Rice

8 SERVINGS

مطبك

M'tabag

This is a Jewish-Iraqi specialty. You cook each ingredient separately and combine them to form a magical dish. *M'tabag* is served as a main meal, accompanied by salad and pickles.

2 teaspoons vegetable oil	½ teaspoon red pepper flakes
2 medium-size onions, sliced	¼ teaspoon ground coriander
1 teaspoon curry powder	½ teaspoon mango powder
1 teaspoon dried dill	Juice of 1 large lemon
½ teaspoon salt	4 large potatoes, boiled, peeled and sliced
½ teaspoon garlic powder	2 pounds fish fillets, such as cod, sole,
½ teaspoon ground cumin	trout, or red snapper
½ teaspoon black pepper	2 cups cooked rice

Put 2 cups of water in a pot and bring to a boil, then reduce heat to medium. Place the fish in a strainer, and suspend the strainer over the boiling water. Cover the strainer with the pot lid and steam the fish until it is tender (about 10 minutes). Mash and set aside.

Preheat the oven to 350°F.

Heat the vegetable oil in a pan over high heat and add the onions. Reduce heat to medium. Stir in the curry, dill, salt, garlic powder, cumin, black pepper, red pepper, coriander, and mango powder. Reduce heat to low. Add the lemon juice, potatoes, fish, mix and simmer for 5 minutes.

Spread the fish and potato mixture evenly in a large, deep baking pan. Top it evenly with the rice.

Bake for 30 minutes. Serve hot.

Rice Dishes

אורז

تمن

T'man

Rice is the most widely used grain in Jewish-Iraqi cuisine. Traditionally, it is always served as part of the main dish, or it can be a meal in itself,

especially when cooked with various additions, such as beans, lentils, meat, chicken, fish, almonds, or raisins. We eat rice every day all year round.

My sister Aya uses the traditional method of cooking rice: She puts it in a pan with cold water, then wraps the lid with a cloth to seal it tightly. The rice is then simmered over a low heat. The slowly cooked rice has great texture and is a pleasure to eat, because the grains do not stick together.

Rice, Garbanzo Beans, and Raisins

بلأؤ أبحمص فقشمش

Plow ab Hmas oo Kishmish

8 SERVINGS

This dish can be made from leftover rice. If you choose to use canned garbanzo beans, skip the soaking and cooking steps. It can be served as a main course, and is especially good with baked chicken or with salad and pickles.

2 cups dried garbanzo beans, or 1 (15-ounce) can	1 medium-size onion, chopped
2 teaspoons vegetable oil	½ teaspoon salt
1 medium-size onion, chopped	½ teaspoon red pepper flakes
2 cups uncooked rice	Juice of 1 large lemon
4 large tomatoes, minced	½ teaspoon garlic powder
½ teaspoon salt	½ cup (about 6 small) chopped button mushrooms
½ teaspoon black pepper	⅔ cup raisins
2 teaspoons vegetable oil	¼ cup almonds, sliced

Cover the garbanzo beans with water and leave to soak overnight in a large bowl. Then drain off the water and add fresh water. Bring to a boil over high heat and cook until the beans are tender (about 45 minutes). Remove from heat, drain off the water again, and set the beans aside in a pan. If using caned beans, just drain and rinse.

Heat 2 teaspoons of the vegetable oil in a pot and add the onion. Add the rice and stir for 2 minutes. Add 4 cups of water, the tomatoes, salt, and black pepper, and bring to a boil. Reduce heat to low. Cover and simmer until the rice is tender (about ½ an hour).

Heat the 2 teaspoons of vegetable oil in a pan over high heat and add the onion. Reduce heat to low. Stir in the salt, red pepper, lemon juice, garlic powder, mushrooms, raisins, almonds, and garbanzo beans. Simmer for 2 minutes. Remove from heat.

Stir the garbanzo bean mixture into the cooked rice. Serve hot or at room temperature.

Rice and Green Lentils

مجدره

Mujadrah

8 SERVINGS

Rice and lentils make a great vegetarian dish, particularly when served hot in the winter, but also throughout the year.

2 teaspoons vegetable oil	½ teaspoon garlic powder
1 medium-size onion, chopped	½ teaspoon ground turmeric
1 cup green lentils	½ teaspoon black pepper
1½ cups rice	1 teaspoon ground cumin
1 teaspoon salt	3 large zucchini, chopped

Heat the vegetable oil in a pot over high heat and add the onion. Stir in the lentils and rice and cook for 2 minutes. Add 4 cups of water, salt, garlic powder, turmeric, black pepper, and cumin, and bring to a boil.

Reduce heat to low. Stir in the zucchini. Cover and simmer until the rice and lentils are tender (about ½ hour).

Rice with String Beans

بلأؤ وُلؤبياً
Plow oo Lubia

The rice in this recipe is enhanced by green beans and red tomatoes, and often garnished with grated carrots.

2 teaspoons olive oil	*½ teaspoon garlic powder*
1 medium-size onion, chopped	*½ teaspoon hot paprika*
2 cups uncooked rice	*½ teaspoon curry powder*
1 (4-ounce) can tomato sauce	*Juice of 1 large lemon*
1 teaspoon dried dill	*1 pound green beans, chopped*
1 teaspoon salt	*2 large tomatoes, minced*

Heat the olive oil in a pot over high heat and add the onion. Add the rice and stir for 2 minutes. Add 3½ cups of water, tomato sauce, dill, salt, garlic powder, paprika, curry, and lemon juice, and bring to a boil. Add the green beans and tomatoes. Reduce heat to low, cover, and simmer until the rice is tender (about ½ hour).

Rice, Onions, and Raisins

بلاُؤ أببصلى ؤقشمش

Plow ab Bassal oo Kishmish

8 SERVINGS

As a leftover, this dish makes a great after school snack. My mother used to stir in one tablespoon of cold water with the rice, heat it over a low flame, and serve it warm. The onions and raisins add sweet flavor to this dish.

2 cups uncooked long-grain rice	*½ teaspoon hot paprika*
1 teaspoon salt	*1 teaspoon mango powder*
2 teaspoons vegetable oil	*½ teaspoon dried oregano*
2 large onions, sliced	*¼ cup chopped fresh mint*
½ teaspoon garlic powder	*¼ cup chives, chopped*
½ teaspoon black pepper	*⅔ cup raisins*

Put the rice, 4 cups of water, and the salt in a pan. Bring to a boil, and then reduce heat to low. Cover and simmer until the rice is tender (about ½ hour).

Heat the vegetable oil in a pot over high heat and add the onion. Stir in the garlic powder, black pepper, red pepper, mango powder, and oregano. Reduce heat to low. Add the mint, chives and raisins, and stir for 1 minute. Remove the onion mixture from heat and stir it into the cooked rice. Serve hot or at room temperature.

Rice with Tomatoes

بلأؤ أحمر

Plow Ahmar

Traditionally, the rice is simmered until it is crisp and golden at the bottom of the pan. It is generally scraped and served on the side. It is considered a delicacy, called *ehkaka*, and is our favorite part of the rice.

---

2 teaspoons vegetable oil

1 medium-size onion, chopped

2 cups uncooked long-grain rice

1 (4-ounce) can tomato sauce

4 large tomatoes, minced

¼ cup chopped fresh cilantro

2 stalks celery, thinly sliced

1 teaspoon salt

1 teaspoon dried dill

½ teaspoon black pepper

½ teaspoon garlic powder

Heat the vegetable oil in a pot over high heat and add the onion. Add the rice and stir for 2 minutes. Add 3½ cups of water, the tomatoes, tomato sauce, cilantro, celery, salt, dill, black pepper, and garlic powder, and bring to a boil. Reduce heat to low. Cover and simmer until the rice is tender (about ½ hour).

Rice and Lentils with Butter

كجرى أبـهن
Kichri ab Dehin

This dish is served as a main course. Top it with plain yogurt, fried fish, or sunny-side-up eggs—it is nourishing, tastes good, and is easy to digest. You may substitute olive oil for the butter.

2 teaspoons olive oil	2 large tomatoes, minced
1 medium-size onion, chopped	1 teaspoon salt
2 cups uncooked rice	½ teaspoon black pepper
1½ cups orange lentils	1 tablespoon butter
1 (4-ounce) can tomato sauce	

Heat the olive oil in a pot over high heat and add the onion. Add the rice and lentils, and stir for 2 minutes. Add 6 cups of water, the tomato sauce, tomatoes, salt, and black pepper, and bring to a boil. Reduce heat to low. Cover and simmer until the rice and lentils are tender (about ½ hour). Melt the butter, pour it over the rice mixture, stir, and serve hot.

Mama Nazima's Jewish-Iraqi Cuisine

Rice and Lentils with Cumin and Garlic

كجرى أبثّوم وُكمؤن

Kichri Thum oo Cumin

This splendid rice and lentil dish is often served with fried fish. When we immigrated to Israel from Iraq, the first meal that my mother cooked for us from our cuisine was *kichri* with cumin. We all devoured it. This is still my favorite meal.

4 teaspoons olive oil	½ teaspoon black pepper
1 medium-size onion, chopped	½ teaspoon paprika
2 cups uncooked rice	8 garlic cloves, crushed
1½ cups orange lentils	1 teaspoon ground cumin
1 teaspoon salt	

Heat 2 teaspoons of the olive oil in a pot over high heat and add the onion. Add the rice and lentils, and stir for 2 minutes. Add 6 cups of water, salt, black pepper, and paprika, and bring to a boil. Reduce heat to low, cover, and simmer until the rice and lentils are tender (about ½ hour).

Heat the remaining 2 teaspoons of olive oil. Reduce heat to low. Add the garlic and cumin, and cook for 1 minute. Stir the oil mixture into the rice and lentils. Serve hot.

Rice with Fava Beans

بلاؤ أببقلى
Plow ab Bakili

This recipe, which is rich in protein and carbohydrates, may be prepared in advance. It is my family's favorite fava bean dish. The herbs and spices produce a great flavor. The turmeric and minced tomatoes provide color and create a pleasant presentation.

2 cups uncooked rice	½ cup chopped fresh parsley
1 (4-ounce) can tomato sauce	2 large tomatoes, diced
1 teaspoon salt	½ teaspoon salt
1 teaspoon black pepper	½ teaspoon black pepper
1 teaspoon turmeric	½ teaspoon hot paprika
4 teaspoons olive oil	1 teaspoon dried oregano
1 medium-size onion, chopped	Juice of 1 large lemon
4 cups fresh fava beans, peeled (see Note, page 77)	

In a pot, combine the rice, 3½ cups of water, the tomato sauce, salt, black pepper, and turmeric, and bring to a boil. Cover and reduce heat to low, and cook until the rice is tender (about ½ hour).

Heat the olive oil in a pan over high heat and add the onion. Reduce heat to medium, add the fava beans and 1 cup of water, cover, and cook until the beans are tender (about 10 minutes). Stir in the parsley, tomatoes, salt, black pepper, paprika, oregano, and lemon juice. Reduce heat to low, cover and simmer for 10 minutes.

Stir the fava bean mixture into the rice. Serve hot or cold.

Breads, Pastries and Rolls

לחמים ממולאים וקאעק

خبز محشى وُكعك

Chubiz M'hshyee oo Kaak

Our cuisine is rich with a variety of pastries,

including *burekas* filled with cheese, meat,

spinach, or potatoes; *sambusak* of all kinds; *kaak*;

and sweets. They can be served as appetizers,

main meals, side dishes, snacks, or desserts.

Garbanzo Bean Turnovers

سمبوسك أبحمص

Sambusak ab Hmas

Turnovers are traditionally prepared for guests and on special occasions. They can be served throughout the day as appetizers, as a lunch meal with various salads and pickles, or as an afternoon snack. You can make large quantities and refrigerate for later.

DOUGH:	STUFFING:
1 (¼-ounce) package active dry yeast	2 cups dried garbanzo beans, soaked
1 teaspoon salt	overnight, or 2 (15-ounce) cans
1 teaspoon baking powder	2 teaspoons vegetable oil
2 teaspoons sugar	2 medium-size onions, chopped
1 cup warm water	½ teaspoon salt
2 cups all-purpose flour	1½ teaspoons ground cumin
	¼ teaspoon ground ginger
	½ teaspoon black pepper
	¼ teaspoon ground nutmeg
	½ teaspoon white pepper
	¼ cup vegetable oil

Put the yeast, salt, baking powder, sugar, and water in a large bowl, stir, and set aside for 15 minutes. Add the flour, mix, and knead until the dough becomes firm. Cover the dough in a bowl and let it rise for 2 hours.

Drain and rinse the garbanzo beans, place in a saucepan, cover with fresh water, and bring to a boil over high heat. Reduce heat to medium. Cook until the beans are tender (about 1 hour). If using canned beans drain and rinse. Mash them with a grinder.

Heat the 2 teaspoons of vegetable oil in a large pan over high heat and add the onions.

CONTINUED

Reduce heat to medium. Stir the salt, cumin, ginger, black pepper, nutmeg, and white pepper into the mashed beans. Reduce heat to low. Simmer for 5 minutes and cool.

Divide the dough into twenty pieces. Roll each into a 3-inch circle. Place 2 tablespoons of the stuffing on each circle. Fold the dough to cover the stuffing. Seal the edges of the *sambusak* by pinching them together with your fingers. The soft, moist dough will stick together. The turnover shapes resemble half-moons.

Heat the remaining ¼ cup of vegetable oil in a large pan over high heat. Reduce heat to medium. Fry each *sambusak* until golden brown on both sides.

Alternately, preheat the oven to 350°F and grease a baking sheet. Place each *sambusak* on the baking sheet and bake until golden brown (about ½ hour).

Meat Turnovers

سمبؤسك أبلحم
Sambusak ab Lahm

These *sambusak* have a delicious flavor and fragrance. They can be served as a main dish with rice, vegetables, and pickles. They also make a great appetizer.

DOUGH:	½ teaspoon salt
1 (¼-ounce) package active dry yeast	½ teaspoon garlic powder
1 teaspoon salt	½ teaspoon black pepper
1 teaspoon baking powder	¼ teaspoon hot paprika
2 teaspoons sugar	1 teaspoon curry powder
1 cup warm water	Juice of 1 large lemon
2 cups all-purpose flour	½ teaspoon ground ginger
	⅔ cup raisins
STUFFING:	¼ cup pine nuts
2 tablespoons vegetable oil	¼ cup chopped fresh basil
1 medium-size onion, chopped	¼ cup vegetable oil
1 stalk celery, chopped	
2 pounds boneless chicken or beef, chopped	

Combine the yeast, salt, baking powder, sugar, and water in a large bowl and set aside for 15 minutes. Add the flour, mix, and knead until the dough becomes firm. Cover and let it rise for 2 hours.

Heat the 2 teaspoons of vegetable oil in a large pan over high heat and add the onion. Add the celery and meat, mix, and cook, strring, until the meat is tender (about 10 minutes). Add the salt, garlic powder, black pepper, red pepper, curry, lemon juice, ginger and mix. Reduce heat to low. Simmer for 2 minutes. Stir in the raisins, pine nuts, and basil, and let cool.

Prepare and cook the *sambusak* as directed on page 152.

Breads, Pastries and Rolls

Feta Cheese Turnovers

سمبؤسك أجبن
Sambusak ab Jibin

This *sambusak* is good as a snack; traditionally it is also served with afternoon tea.

DOUGH:	**STUFFING:**
1 (¼-ounce) package active dry yeast	1 (8-ounce) package cream cheese
1 teaspoon salt	1 (8-ounce) container ricotta cheese
1 teaspoon baking powder	1 (8-ounce) container crumbled feta
2 teaspoons sugar	cheese
1 cup warm water	2 eggs, lightly beaten
2 cups all-purpose flour	2 teaspoons vegetable oil
	4 teaspoons sesame seeds

Combine the yeast, salt, baking powder, sugar, water in a large bowl and set aside for 15 minutes. Add the flour, mix and knead until the dough becomes firm. Cover and let it rise for 2 hours.

STUFFING:

Put the cream cheese, ricotta cheese, feta cheese and eggs in a bowl, mix, and refrigerate for ½ hour.

Preheat oven at 350°F and grease a baking sheet.

Prepare the *sambusak* as direct-ed on page 152.

Place the *sambusak* neatly on the prepared baking sheet, sprinkle the sesame seeds on top, and bake until golden brown (about ½ hour).

Potato Pie

בורקס עם תפוחי אדמה

Burekas im Tapuhe Adama

Burekas were not originated by the Iraqi Jews; rather they were brought to Israel by immigrants from various other countries, such as Turkey and Greece. We adapted this dish and modified it to fit our cuisine.

6 large potatoes	¼ teaspoon ground coriander
4 teaspoons vegetable oil	2 stalks celery, chopped
2 medium-size onions, chopped	½ cup chopped green chile peppers
1 teaspoon curry powder	2 large tomatoes, chopped
½ teaspoon garlic powder	¼ cup chopped fresh basil
Juice of 1 large lemon	8 ounces Cheddar cheese
½ teaspoon ground ginger	1 pound phyllo dough, thawed
½ teaspoon paprika	

Put the potatoes in a large pot and cover with water. Boil until the potatoes are tender. Drain off the water, peel the potatoes, and chop.

Heat 2 teaspoons of the vegetable oil in a large pan over high heat and add the onions. Reduce heat to low. Stir in the curry, garlic powder, lemon juice, ginger, paprika, and coriander. Add the celery and simmer for 2 minutes. Add the potatoes, chile, tomatoes, and basil. Simmer for 2 minutes and cool. Stir in the Cheddar cheese.

Preheat the oven to 350°F and grease a large baking sheet.

Place ten sheets of the phyllo dough evenly on the prepared baking sheet. Pour the potato mixture on top the dough and spread evenly. Top the potato with twelve layers of the phyllo dough. Brush the top with the remaining 2 teaspoons of the vegetable oil. Cut into forty squares.

Bake until golden brown (about 60 minutes). Serve hot or cold.

Breads, Pastries and Rolls

Phyllo Cheese Pie

בורקס עם גבינה

Burekas im Gevina

Amongst my guests this dish has been one of the most popular *burekas*. It is prepared with low-fat cheese and served hot or cold, either as a meal with salad, or as a dessert sprinkled with powdered sugar or honey. It is suitable for freezing. When you are ready to bake it, remove it from the freezer and immediately bake at 350°F until golden brown (about 75 minutes).

---

1 (8-ounce) package cream cheese	½ cup milk
1 (8-ounce) container cottage cheese	3 eggs, lightly beaten
1 (8-ounce) container ricotta cheese	2 teaspoons vegetable oil
8 ounces mozzarella cheese	1 pound phyllo dough, thawed

Combine the cream cheese, cottage cheese, ricotta cheese, mozzarella cheese, milk, and eggs in a large bowl, and chill for 15 minutes.

Preheat the oven to 350°F

Grease a large baking sheet. Place ten layers of phyllo dough evenly on the prepared greased baking sheet. Pour the cheese mixture on top of the dough, and spread it evenly. Top the cheese with twelve layers of phyllo. Brush the upper layer of dough with the vegetable oil. Cut into forty squares.

Bake until golden brown (about 60 minutes). Serve hot or cold.

Feta and Spinach Pie

בורקס עם גבינה ותרד

Burekas im Gevina veh Tered

Phyllo dough can be found in almost any grocery store. You need to prepare the *burekas* quickly so the dough does not dry out. If the sheets of dough begin to dry, you may spray them lightly with water. For the best presentation, cut the dough before baking, because crispy phyllo breaks unevenly after baking.

2 teaspoons olive oil	2 pounds spinach, stemmed and chopped
2 medium-size onions, chopped	1 pound feta cheese, grated
¼ teaspoon ground nutmeg	½ cup roasted green chile peppers
½ teaspoon garlic powder	1/4 cup chopped fresh basil
½ teaspoon ground ginger	2 teaspoons olive oil
½ teaspoon ground cumin	1 pound phyllo dough, thawed

Heat the olive oil in a pan over high heat and add the onions. Reduce heat to low. Stir in the nutmeg, garlic powder, ginger, and cumin. Add the spinach, mix and cook for 10 minutes. Remove from heat and cool, then add the grated feta cheese, chile peppers, and basil.

Preheat the oven to 350°F

Grease a large baking sheet. Place ten sheets of the phyllo dough evenly on the prepared greased baking sheet. Pour the cheese mixture on top of the dough and spread evenly. Top the cheese with twelve sheets of phyllo. Brush the upper layer dough with the olive oil. Cut into forty rectangles.

Bake until golden brown (about 60 minutes). Serve hot or cold.

Iraqi Pita Bread

عيش تذؤر
Aish Tanure

20 PIECES

I remember my father saying that there is something deeply satisfying about inhaling the aroma of freshly baked bread. He put a piece of cheese or leftover meat on the bread, topped it with salad and pickles, and rolled it over to make a wrap sandwich. This sandwich is called *lafa*, and is my children's favorite snack.

1 (¼-ounce) package active dry yeast	1 cup warm water
1 teaspoon salt	2 tablespoons vegetable oil
1 teaspoon baking powder	2 cups all-purpose flour
2 teaspoons sugar	½ cup whole wheat flour

Combine the yeast, salt, baking powder, sugar, water, and oil in a large bowl, mix, and set aside for 15 minutes. Add both flours, and knead until the dough becomes firm. Cover and let it rise for 2 hours.

Preheat the oven to 400°F and grease a large baking sheet.

Divide the dough into twenty pieces. Flatten each piece and roll into a ¼-inch-thick circle. Place as many pieces as can fit on the sheet, and bake until golden brown (about 10 minutes). Serve hot or cold.

158   *Mama Nazima's Jewish-Iraqi Cuisine*

Bread with Spices

خبز أبزعتر وُسمق

Chubiz ab Zaatar oo Sumack

The spices used in this bread are *zaatar* and *sumack*. *Zaatar* is the Arabic word for ground thyme. *Sumack* is a spice derived from the berries of a bush that grows wild in all Mediterranean areas. The berries are dried and crushed to form a coarse purple-red powder. It has a sour taste.

DOUGH:	STUFFING:
1 (¼-ounce) package active dry yeast	4 teaspoons olive oil
1 teaspoon salt	3 tablespoons zaatar
1 teaspoon baking powder	3 tablespoons sumack
2 teaspoons sugar	
1 cup warm water	
2 cups whole wheat flour	

Combine the yeast, salt, baking powder, sugar, and water in a large bowl, and set aside for 15 minutes. Add the flour and knead until the dough becomes firm. Cover and let it rise for 2 hours.

Divide the dough into two pieces.

Preheat the oven to 350°F and grease the large baking sheets.

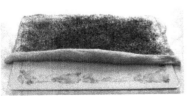

Flatten each half of the dough and roll it into a ¼-inch thick circle. Brush the top of each circle with 2 teaspoons of olive oil and sprinkle each top with the 1½ tablespoons of the *zaatar* and 1½ tablepoons of the *sumack*. Roll up the dough, covering all spices, to make a cylindrical shape. Seal the edges of the dough by pinching them together with your fingers. The soft moist dough will stick together.

Place the loaves on the baking sheets and bake until golden brown (about ½ hour).

Iraqi Pancakes

كأهى
Kahi

Kahi are traditionally served at breakfast on the first morning after the end of Passover. This leavened bread marks the end of the holiday and the beginning of ordinary days. Today, *kahi* are served at various other occasions, especially when my children are craving them.

1 (¼-ounce) package active dry yeast	1 cup warm water
1 teaspoon salt	2 cups all-purpose flour
1 teaspoon baking powder	3 tablespoons vegetable oil
2 teaspoons sugar	

Combine the yeast, salt, baking powder, sugar, and water in a large bowl, and set aside for 15 minutes. Add the flour and knead until the dough becomes firm. Cover and let rise for 2 hours.

Divide the dough into twenty pieces. Flatten each piece and roll into a ¼-inch-thick circle.

Heat the vegetable oil in a large pan over high heat. Reduce heat to medium. Fry each piece of dough until golden brown on both sides. If your pan is large enough, you can fry more than one *kahi* at a time.

Serve hot or cold with sugar, powdered sugar, honey, or jam.

Mama Nazima's Jewish-Iraqi Cuisine

Sesame Rolls

كعك أبسمسم

Kaak ab Sumsum

Kaak are easy to make. They are small and have a unique nutty taste that goes well with tea or coffee.

---

1 (¼-ounce) package active dry yeast	¼ cup vegetable oil
1 teaspoon baking powder	1½ cups all-purpose flour
2 teaspoons sugar	2 cups whole wheat flour
2 teaspoons salt	1 teaspoon olive oil
1½ cups warm water	4 teaspoons sesame seeds
1 egg, lightly beaten	

Combine the yeast, baking powder, sugar, salt, water, egg, and vegetable oil in a large bowl. Add both flours and knead until the dough becomes firm. Cover and let it rise for 2 hours.

Preheat the oven at 350°F and grease a large baking sheet.

Divide the dough into fifty pieces. Roll each piece into a 6-inch-long rope and pinch the ends together to make a circle. Place the *kaak* neatly on a tray and brush them with the olive oil. Sprinkle the *kaak* with the sesame seeds, and bake until golden brown (about 20 minutes).

Apple Cinnamon Rolls

كعك أبيهلُرأت ؤتفلُح

Kaak Beharat oo Tefach

These rolls have great flavor and aroma. As children we liked to eat them, brushed with honey and sprinkled with ground almonds.

1 (¼-ounce) package active dry yeast	¼ cup honey
1 teaspoon baking powder	1 teaspoon ground cinnamon
2 teaspoons sugar	½ teaspoon ground cardamom
1 teaspoon salt	1½ cups all-purpose flour
1 cup warm water	
1 egg, lightly beaten	2 cups whole wheat flour
¼ cup vegetable oil	1 teaspoon olive oil
3 large green apples, peeled and grated	4 teaspoons sesame seeds

Combine the yeast, baking powder, sugar, salt, water, egg, and vegetable oil in a large bowl. Stir in the apples, honey, cinnamon, and cardamom. For a different taste, you may substitute half a teaspoon of ground cumin and half a teaspoon of ground coriander for thecinnamon.

Add both flours, and knead until the dough becomes firm. Cover, set aside, and let it rise for 2 hours.

Preheat oven to 350°F and grease a large baking sheet.

Divide the dough into fifty pieces. Roll each piece into a 6-inch-long rope and pinch the ends together to make a circle. Place the *kaak* neatly on the baking sheet. Brush the *kaak* with the olive oil. Sprinkle the *kaak* with the sesame seeds, and bake until golden brown (about 20 minutes).

Raisin Rolls

קעק עם צמוקים
Kaak eem Tzmukin

MAKES 50 ROLLS

A variation on this dish involves adding one-quarter cup of lemon juice to the dough; my mother's innovation. According to her, lemon makes the food easier to digest. Of course, it also gives the *kaak* a light lemony taste.

1 (¼-ounce) package active dry yeast	1 teaspoon ground cinnamon
1 teaspoon baking powder	2/3 cup raisins
2 teaspoons sugar	3 tablespoons honey
1 teaspoon salt	1½ cups all-purpose flour
1 cup warm water	2 cups whole wheat flour
1 egg, lightly beaten	1 teaspoon olive oil
¼ cup vegetable oil	4 teaspoons sesame seeds
½ teaspoon ground cardamom	

Combine the yeast, baking powder, sugar, salt, water, egg, and vegetable oil in a bowl. Add the cardamom, cinnamon, raisins, honey and mix. Add both flours, mix, and knead until the dough becomes firm. Cover, set aside and let it rise for 2 hours.

Preheat the oven to 350°F and grease a large baking sheet.

Divide the dough into fifty pieces. Roll each piece into a 6-inch-long rope and pinch the ends together to make a circle. Place the *kaak* neatly on the baking sheet. Brush the *kaak* with the olive oil. Sprinkle the *kaak* with the sesame seeds, and bake until golden brown (about 20 minutes).

Desserts

حألؤأت ؤمربة

Halawat

The Iraqi Jews make use of what the environment offers to make desserts and jams from a variety of fruits, some vegetables, and multiple types of nuts. The ingredients for these recipes therefore include berries, oranges, quinces, coconut, lemons, dates, pumpkins, almonds, pecans, walnuts, and pistachios.

Date Cookies

بعبع أبتمر
Baobaoh ab Tam'r

In Jewish-Iraqi cuisine, emphasis is placed on dates, because a variety of dates grow in Iraq, especially in the southern region. As a child, I remember date palm trees along the river. Everywhere dates were carried in large, woven baskets. Many dishes and desserts are made from them, including pitted dates stuffed with walnuts and almonds, and a special type of honey, *silan*, extracted from dates.

1 (¼-ounce) package active dry yeast	1 teaspoon ground cinnamon
1 teaspoon baking powder	1 teaspoon ground ginger
2 teaspoons sugar	1½ cups all-purpose flour
1 teaspoon salt	2 cups whole wheat flour
1 cup warm water	1 pound dates, pitted
4 teaspoons vegetable oil	1 egg, lightly beaten
¼ teaspoon ground cardamom	4 teaspoons sesame seeds

Combine the yeast, baking powder, sugar, salt, water, and 2 tablespoons of the vegetable oil in a bowl. Add the cardamom, cinnamon, and ginger. Stir in both flours, and knead until the dough becomes firm. Cover, set aside, and let it rise for 2 hours.

Heat the remaining 2 teaspoons of vegetable oil in a pan over low heat. Add the dates, stir, and mash until they become soft. Remove from heat and cool.

Preheat the oven to 350°F and grease a large baking sheet.

Divide the dough into thirty pieces. Roll each piece into a 2-inch-circle. Place 1 teaspoon of the date mixture in the center of each circle. Fold the dough to cover the stuffing. Seal the edges of the *baobaoh* by pinching them together with your fingers. The soft moist dough will stick together. Roll the dough to make a ball and flatten each ball to form a circle. Place the *baobaoh* on the baking sheet. Brush each cookie with the egg and then sprinkle with sesame seeds. Bake until golden brown (about 20 minutes).

"Kaser al sultan oo mithal cochy makan" ("The king's palace is not like my little hut") means that a person can only find true freedom in his own home.

Desserts   167

Date Turnovers

سمبؤسك أبتمر

Sambusak ab Tam'r

Dates are a tasty fruit, rich in nutrients, rendering immediate satisfaction to a hungry person. When they are blended with spices, they make flavorful snacks and desserts.

DOUGH:	
1 (¼-ounce) package active dry yeast	**STUFFING:**
1 teaspoon baking powder	*2 teaspoons vegetable oil*
1 teaspoon salt	*1 pound pitted dates*
1 cup warm water	*½ teaspoon ground cardamom*
½ teaspoon ground cinnamon	*½ teaspoon ground ginger*
¼ cup sugar	*Juice of 2 large lemons*
¼ cup honey	
1 cup all-purpose flour	*1 egg , lightly beaten*
2 cups whole wheat flour	*4 teaspoons sesame seeds*

Combine the yeast, baking powder, salt, water and cinnamon, in a bowl. Stir in the sugar, and honey. Add both flours, and knead until the dough becomes firm. Cover, set aside, and let rise for 2 hours.

Preheat the oven to 350°F and grease a large baking pan.

Heat 2 teaspoons of the vegetable oil in a pan over a low flame. Add the dates, cardamom, ginger, and lemon juice and stir, and mash until they form a puree. Remove from heat and cool.

Divide the dough into fifty pieces. Roll each piece to make a 2-inch circle. Place ½ teaspoon of the cooked dates in the center of each circle. Fold the dough to cover the stuffing. Seal the edges of the *sambusak* by pinching them together with your fingers. The soft moist dough will stick together. The turnovers will resemble half-moons.

Place all of the *sambusak* neatly on the prepared greased baking pan. Brush each *sambusak* with the egg, and sprinkle with sesame seeds. Bake until golden brown (about 20 minutes).

Date-Almond Balls

تمر أبلؤز

Tam'r ab Loze

MAKES 40 BALLS

Date-almond balls make a bite-size dessert. Alternately, you can spread the mashed date mixture on a cake and garnish with almonds.

1 tablespoon vegetable oil	¼ teaspoon ground cardamom
2 pounds unpitted dates	40 whole almonds
1 tablespoon fresh lemon juice	1 cup shredded sweetened coconut
1 tablespoon rose water	

Heat the vegetable oil in a pan over low heat. Add the dates, stirring and mashing until they become soft. Stir in the lemon juice, rose water, and cardamom. Remove from heat and cool.

Put water in a second bowl. Dip your hands in the water so that the dates will not stick to them.

Divide the date mixture into forty pieces. Flatten each piece, place an almond in the center, and roll to make a ball, covering the almond.

Spread the coconut on a cookie sheet. Roll each date ball in the coconut until covered. Place the date balls on a serving platter and refrigerate for ½ hour.

A Lamp

In the early stages of the birth of Israel, lamps like the one shown below lit the homes of many immigrants. There were limited resources, then and such public utilities as gas and electricity were not yet developed.

As a child, when the world around me was asleep, I dimmed the light so it shone only on my book. The light played with the shadows that formed in the room, and I thought that it was magic. Recently, I found an identical lamp on the shelf of a gift shop in Fisherman's Wharf, Monterey, California. Now the lamp is sitting in my living room, keeping the magical memory alive.

Desserts

169

Lemon Ginger Cookies

بعبع حلؤ

Baobaoh H'loo

Preparing these cookies is a great way to get children involved in baking. They are easy to make and fun to eat - my children's favorite after school snack.

1 (¼-ounce) package active dry yeast	¼ teaspoon ground cardamom
1 teaspoon baking powder	1 teaspoon ground ginger
1 teaspoon salt	1 teaspoon ground cinnamon
1 cup sugar	½ cup chopped almonds
1 cup warm water	1½ cups all-purpose flour
Juice of 2 large lemons	2 cups whole wheat flour
½ cup honey	1 egg, lightly beaten
2 tablespoons vegetable oil	4 teaspoons sesame seeds

Combine the yeast, baking powder, salt, sugar, water, lemon juice, honey, and vegetable oil in a bowl. Add the cardamom, ginger, cinnamon, and almonds. Stir in both flours and knead until the dough becomes firm. Cover, set aside, and let it rise for 2 hours.

Preheat the oven to 350°F. Grease a large baking sheet.

Divide the dough into fifty pieces and flatten into 2-inch circles. Place the cookies on a prepared greased baking sheet. Brush each cookie with the egg, and sprinkle the cookies with the sesame seeds. Bake until golden brown (about 20 minutes).

Mama Nazima's Jewish-Iraqi Cuisine

Nut and Honey Turnovers

سمبؤسك أبعسلى ؤلؤز

Sambusak ab Assal oo Loze

The nutty sweetness of this dish is heightened by the lemon, ginger, and cardamom in it.

DOUGH:

1 (¼-ounce) package active dry yeast
1 teaspoon baking powder
1 teaspoon salt
1 cup plus 2 tablespoons sugar
½ cup plus 2 tablespoons honey
1 cup warm water

STUFFING:

½ teaspoon ground cinnamon
1 cup all-purpose flour
2 cups whole wheat flour
1 cup chopped almonds
1 cup chopped walnuts
Juice of 2 large lemons
½ teaspoon ground ginger
½ teaspoon ground cardamom
2 teaspoons vegetable oil
1 egg, lightly beaten

Combine the yeast, baking powder, salt, 2 teaspoons of the sugar, 2 tablespoons of the honey, water and cinnamon, in a bowl. Add both flours and knead until the dough becomes firm. Cover, set aside, and let it rise for 2 hours.

In a second bowl combine ½ cup water, the almonds, walnuts, the remaining 1 cup of sugar, the remaining ½ cup of honey, lemon juice, ginger, and cardamom.

Preheat the oven to 350°F and grease a large baking sheet.

Divide the dough to fifty pieces. Roll each piece into a 2-inch circle and put 1 tablespoon of nut stuffing in the center. Fold the dough to cover the stuffing. Seal the edges of the *sambusak* by pinching them together with your fingers. The soft moist dough will stick together. The turnovers will shaped like half-moons.

Place the cookies on the prepared baking sheet. Brush each cookie with the egg, and bake until golden brown (about 20 minutes).

Baklavah

بقلأؤه
Baklawah

My mother modified the traditional recipe into a low-fat *baklavah*. No butter is used between the layers; the entire recipe contains just 4 teaspoons of oil.

3 cups pecans or walnuts, chopped	**SYRUP:**
4 cups almonds, chopped	1 cup sugar
2 cups unsalted shelled pistachios, chopped	½ cup honey
1 cup sugar	Juice of 2 large lemons
½ teaspoon ground cinnamon	2 tablespoons rose water
½ teaspoon ground ginger	½ teaspoon ground ginger
½ teaspoon ground cardamom	½ teaspoon ground cinnamon
2 tablespoons rose water	½ teaspoon ground cardamom
Juice of 1 large lemon	
½ cup honey	4 teaspoons vegetable oil
	1 pound phyllo dough, thawed

Combine the walnuts, almonds, pistachios, sugar, cinnamon, ginger, cardamom, rose water, lemon juice, honey, and ½ cup of water.

Combine 1 cup of water, the sugar, honey, lemon juice, rose water, ginger, cinnamon, and cardamom in a pot. Cook over low heat, stirring and bringing to a boil. Remove from heat and cool.

Preheat the oven to 350°F and grease a large baking sheet with 2 teaspoons of the vegetable oil.

Stack 10 layers of the phyllo dough evenly on the tray. Place the nut stuffing on top of the phyllo layers and spread evenly. Cover with the remaining dough. Brush the upper surface of the dough with the remaining 2 teaspoons of the vegetable oil.

Cut into fifty squares or diamonds. Bake the *baklavah* until golden brown (about ½ hour). Remove the *baklavah* from the oven and pour the syrup over it. Cool and refrigerate.

Phyllo Nut Rolls

ملفّف
Malfufe

Many adults are trying to cut down on fat in their diets. Traditionally, *malfufe* are made by spreading butter between layers of the phyllo dough. In this recipe, the fat is reduced. One can still enjoy the taste of the nuts even when butter is not added between the layers of dough.

3 cups walnuts, chopped	½ teaspoon ground cardamom
4 cups almonds, chopped	Juice of 2 large lemons
2 cups unsalted shelled pistachios, chopped	2 tablespoons rose water
1 cup sugar	½ cup honey
½ teaspoon ground cinnamon	1 pound phyllo dough, thawed
½ teaspoon ground ginger	1 tablespoon vegetable oil

Combine the chopped walnuts, almonds, pistachios, sugar, cinnamon, ginger, cardamom, lemon juice, rose water, honey, and ½ cup of water in a pot.

Preheat the oven to 350°F and grease a large baking sheet.

Cut each sheet of phyllo dough in half and put one tablespoon of stuffing in the center. Spread the nut stuffing evenly along the width of the sheet. Fold the

edges in and roll up the dough into a cylinder. Brush each roll lengthwise with vegetable oil.

Place the *malfufe* on a baking tray. Bake until golden brown (about 20 minutes).

Sephardic Doughnuts

زنكؤلة
Zingulah

Zingulah is one of desserts prepared for the holiday of Purim, which occurs in March. Although many desserts are served for this holiday, *zingulah* is usually my children's favorite.

For best results, pour cold syrup over the warm *zingulah*—it cools and keeps the *zingulah* crisp.

DOUGH:

2 cups warm water
1 (¼-ounce) package active dry yeast
1 teaspoon baking powder
1 tablespoon sugar
1 tablespoon honey
1 teaspoon salt
1 teaspoon ground ginger
½ teaspoon ground cinnamon
1½ cups all-purpose flour

2 cups whole wheat flour
2 tablespoons vegetable oil

SYRUP:

1 cup sugar
½ cup honey
Juice of 2 large lemons
2 tablespoons rose water
½ teaspoon ground cardamom

Combine the water, yeast, baking powder, sugar, honey, salt, ginger, and cinnamon, in a large bowl. Stir in both flours and mix.

Heat the vegetable oil in a skillet over high heat. Reduce heat to medium, then pour tablespoons of the dough with a circular motion to make spiral shapes. Fry until golden brown on both sides.

In a pot combine 1½ cups of water, the sugar, honey, lemon juice, rose water, and cardamom. Bring to a boil over low heat. Remove from heat and cool.

Pour the syrup over the *zingulah* while they are still hot. Serve immediately and keep the remainder in the refrigerator.

174

Mama Nazima's Jewish-Iraqi Cuisine

Candied
Almond-Coconut

لُؤزِينأ أَبجؤْز وَحؤْخ

Luzinah Loze oo Choch

MAKES 50 *LUZINAH*

My kids love these *luzinah* because they crunch when bitten into. I love them, because they are easy to make.

---

4 cups almonds, chopped
1½ cups unsalted peanuts, chopped
½ cup sugar
1/4 cup honey
Juice of 2 large lemons
2 tablespoons rose water
grated skin of 1 lemon
grated skin of 1 small orange
1 teaspoon ground cinnamon
½ teaspoon ground cardamom
1 cup shredded sweetened coconut

SYRUP:
½ cup sugar
¼ cup honey
2 tablespoons rose water
Juice of 1 large lemon
½ teaspoon ground ginger
¼ teaspoon ground cloves

Combine the almonds, peanuts, sugar, honey, lemon juice, rose water, lemon zest, orange zest, cinnamon, and cardamom in a bowl.

Put ½ cup of water in a second bowl. Dip your hands into the water so that the nut mixture will not stick to them. Divide the nut mixture into fifty pieces. With wet fingers form 2-inch balls. Spread the coconut evenly over a large serving plate, roll each *luzinah* in the coconut, and set aside on a platter.

SYRUP:
Combine 1 cup of water, the sugar, honey, rose water, lemon juice, ginger, and cloves in a pot, bring to a boil, and cool.

Pour the syrup on a large serving platter. Place the *luzinah* neatly on top of the syrup and chill for about ½ hour.

Candied Orange

لؤزينأ أبيرتقالى
Luzinah ab Portkal

MAKES 30 *LUZINAH*

Israel exports oranges, which are renowned as being sweet and delicious. My family prepares many dishes from oranges: salads, in various desserts such as in this recipe, or garnished with grated chocolate and sprinkled with pistachio nuts.

4 large oranges	*½ teaspoon ground cardamom*
1 large lemon	*1 teaspoon ground cinnamon*
1 cup sugar	*1 cup shredded sweetened coconut*
1 cup honey	

Remove the skin from one of the oranges and the lemon, and set aside. Juice the lemon. Peel all the oranges and remove the seeds. Cut the oranges into small pieces. Combine the cut oranges, the lemon juice, sugar, honey, cardamom, cinnamon, and the orange and lemon skins in a pot. Cook over low heat, stirring, for 5 minutes. Remove from heat.

Spread ½ cup of the shredded coconut evenly over a serving platter. Spread the orange mixture evenly on top of the coconut. Sprinkle the remaining ½ cup of coconut over the orange mixture. Chill for 2 hours and cut into thirty squares.

Candied Quince

لؤزينأ أبحؤه

Luzinah ab Hawah

Luzinah quince or the *luzinah* made from other fruits are traditionally served at weddings and special occasions.

4 large quinces, cleaned and chopped	*1 teaspoon ground cinnamon*
1 cup sugar	*½ teaspoon ground cardamom*
1 cup honey	*½ cup chopped almonds*
Juice of 2 large lemons	*1 cup shredded sweetened coconut*

Put the quinces in a pot with 1 cup of water. Bring to a boil over high heat. Reduce heat to low and cook until the quinces are tender (about 10 minutes). Remove from heat and mash. Add the sugar, honey, lemon juice, cinnamon, and cardamom. Cook over low heat and stir for 5 minutes. Remove from heat, and add the almonds.

Spread ½ cup of the coconut evenly over a large serving platter. Spread the quince mixture evenly on top of the coconut. Sprinkle the remaining ½ cup of coconut over the quince mixture. Chill for 2 hours and cut into thirty squares.

Almond-Pistachio Cookies

شكرلمأ

Shakrlama

These cookies have a very definite citrus flavor of their own; the orange and lemon juices tantalizingly blend with the nuts and spices to enhance one's appetite. *Shakrlama* is a very popular dessert, tasty and easy to digest.

3 cups all-purpose flour	½ teaspoon vanilla extract
1 teaspoon baking powder	1 egg, lightly beaten
1 cup chopped almonds	2 tablespoons vegetable oil
1 cup chopped unsalted pistachios	1 cup sugar
1½ cups fresh orange juice	½ cup honey
Juice of 2 large lemons	40 whole almonds
1 tablespoon rose water	
½ teaspoon ground cardamom	

Combine the flour, baking powder, chopped almonds and pistachios. Stir in the orange juice, lemon juice, rose water, cardamom, and vanilla. Add the egg, oil, sugar, and honey, and mix to make the dough.

Preheat the oven to 350°F and grease a large baking sheet.

Divide the dough into forty pieces, roll each piece into a ball, and flatten slightly. Place an almond in the center of each cookie. Place the *shakrlama* on a prepared sheet and bake until golden brown (about 20 minutes).

Candied Orange Peel with Pistachios

قشـغ برتقألٰ حلٔؤ
Kesher Portkal H'loo

Sweet orange skin provides a great display to bring to the table. When blended with pistachio, it makes a delicious after-dinner dessert or can be served with afternoon tea.

4 large oranges	*¼ teaspoon ground cardamom*
1 large lemon	*1 tablespoon rose water*
1 cup sugar	*1 cup chopped pistachios*
½ cup honey	

Peel the oranges with your hands, cut their skins into large pieces, and set aside.

Juice the remainder of the oranges. Skin the lemon, and then juice it.

Put the orange peels, orange juice, lemon skin, lemon juice, sugar, honey, cardamom, and rose water in a pan. Cook over low heat for 10 minutes.

Spread the chopped pistachio evenly over a cookie sheet. Roll each piece of the orange peel in the pistachios until covered.

Place the pieces of orange peel on a serving platter and refrigerate for ½ hour.

Desserts

179

Pecan-Honey Spread

جؤز ؤسيلأن

Loze oo Silan

Silan is extracted from dates and is similar in consistency to honey. Although served throughout the year, it is made particularly during Passover. One of the most traditional dishes for Passover is *haroset*, which in Iraq consisted of *silan*, ground walnuts, and almonds. In the United States we substitute honey for *silan* and mix it with various ground nuts. *Haroset* is spread on matzoh to make an enjoyable dessert for the Passover holiday.

3 cups pecans, chopped	1½ cups honey
2 cups almonds, chopped	1 tablespoon rose water
Juice of 1 large lemon	

Combine the chopped pecans, almonds, lemon juice, honey, and rose water in a bowl, and chill for ½ hour.

These pages tell the story of Passover, the exodus of the Jews from Egypt. They are of special interest because the story is told in both languages: Hebrew and Jewish Arabic.

Jams

ריבות

مربة

M'rabah

Jams are very popular in Jewish-Iraqi cuisine; they are used everyday in snacks with fresh bread and crackers, or served with afternoon tea. Traditionally, they are cooked from a variety of fruits and vegetables, slowly simmered with honey, lemon juice and rose water, with spices such as cardamom, cinnamon, ginger, and nutmeg added to create a fabulous flavor. When my mother made orange marmalade, she saved the extra orange peels in a bag and stored them in the refrigerator; after she had col-

lected a large quantity, she candied them as in the recipe on page 176.

Pumpkin Preserves

مربة أبقرع

M'rabah ab Kara

2 (16-OUNCE) JARS

Pumpkin, which is used in many Jewish Iraqi recipes, is rich in vitamins and minerals. One of my daughter Liliana's favorite desserts is a sliced banana topped with pumpkin preserves and sprinkled with grated pistachios or grated almonds.

4 lemons	*½ cup honey*
1½ pounds fresh pumpkin, peeled and	*1½ teaspoons ground cinnamon*
cubed	*1 teaspoon ground ginger*
1 cup sugar	*1 tablespoon rose water*

Grate the skin from 2 of the lemons and juice all 4 lemons. Put the pumpkin, lemon skin and juice, and 1½ cups of water in a pan, mix and bring to a boil over high heat. Reduce heat to medium. Cook until the pumpkin is tender (about 10 minutes). Remove from heat. Stir in the sugar, honey, cinnamon, and ginger, and

mash the pumpkin with a large fork until it becomes smooth. Simmer over low heat for for 15 minutes. Remove from heat and stir in the rose water. Chill the pumpkin, transfer into the sanitized jars (see sidebar for instructions), seal, and refrigerate. When refrigerated, pumpkin preserves last for a month.

Sanitization of Glass Jars

Clean the jars with soap and water, and rinse well. In a large pot bring water to a boil over high heat. Reduce heat to low and add the jars so the water level is at least 1 inch above the jars, and add the lids. Boil for ten minutes, remove from heat, and cool.

Jams

183

Quince Jam

Quince jam was a favorite after-school snack of my children. We spread the jam on biscuits or unsalted crackers, topped it with whipped cream, and garnished it with cherries or grapes. It still makes a delicious snack or dessert.

4 large quinces, peeled and cubed	Juice of 2 large lemons
1 black tea bag	½ teaspoon ground cardamom
1 cup sugar	1 tablespoon rose water
½ cup honey	

Put the quinces, the tea bag, and 2 cups of water in a pot, and bring to a boil over high heat. Cook until the quinces are tender (about 15 minutes).

Remove from heat, drain off the water, and discard the tea bag. Mash the quinces in a bowl with a large fork until the fruit becomes smooth. Stir in the sugar, honey, lemon juice, cardamom, rose water, and ½ cup of water, and simmer over low heat for 10 minutes. Remove from heat, chill, and transfer to the sanitized jars (see page 183.) Seal the jars and refrigerate. Quince jam keeps for 2 months.

Orange-Lemon Marmalade

مربة أبرتقأﻟى ﻭﻟمؤن

M'rabah ab Portkal oo Lemon

2 (10-OUNCE) JARS

Orange-lemon marmalade is often enjoyed in my home; spread it on a cake and top it with chocolate frosting, or serve it with crackers and cheese. My husband Bob's favorite combination is marmalade with feta cheese.

6 large oranges	½ cup honey
2 large lemons	1 tablespoon rose water
1 cup sugar	½ teaspoon ground cloves

Grate the skin from 2 of the oranges and set aside. Peel the remaining 4 oranges, slice all 6 oranges, and remove the seeds. Grate the skin from the lemon and set aside. Slice the lemons and remove the seeds. Combine the lemon skin, orange skin, orange slices, lemon slices, 1 cup of water, sugar, honey, rose water, and cloves in a pan, and bring to a boil over high heat. Reduce heat to low and simmer for 15 minutes.

Remove from heat, chill, and transfer to the sanitized jars (see page 183). Seal the jars and refrigerate. Oramge-Lemon Marmalade keeps for 2 months.

Berry Conserve

ריבת תותים
Ribat Tootim

My daughter Liat makes a quick lunch with cottage cheese and berry conserve, decorated with seasonal fruit and served with toasted bread.

3 cups strawberries, stemmed and chopped	½ cup honey
2 cups fresh blueberries	Juice of 2 large lemons
2½ cups fresh raspberries	½ teaspoon ground cinnamon
1 cup sugar	¼ teaspoon ground nutmeg

Combine the strawberries, blueberries, raspberries, 1 cup of water, sugar, honey, lemon juice, cinnamon, and nutmeg in a pot. Bring to a boil over high heat. Reduce heat to low and simmer for 15 minutes. Remove from heat, chill, and transfer to the sanitized jars. (see page 183). Seal the jars and refrigerate. Berry Conserve keeps for 2 months.

Apple-Pear Marmalade

M'rabah ab Tufach oo Armute

Apple pear marmalade is served with *gawrag*, toasted Jewish-Iraqi bread (page 158). *Gawrag* is made by placing the bread at 200°F in a preheated oven until it becomes dark brown. My son Nir loves the crunchy texture and the sweet and delicate taste.

4 large green apples, peeled and chopped	½ teaspoon ground cinnamon
4 large pears, peeled and chopped	2 tablespoons rose water
Skin and juice of 1 large orange	1 cup sugar
Juice of 1 large lemon	1 cup honey
½ teaspoon ground ginger	

Combine the apples, pears, orange zest, orange juice, lemon juice, ginger, cinnamon, rose water, sugar, and honey in a pot. Add 1½ cups of water and bring to a boil over high heat. Reduce heat to low and simmer for 15 minutes. Remove from heat, chill, and transfer to the sanitized jars (see page 183). Seal the jars and refrigerate. Apple-Pear Marmalade keeps for 2 months.

Jams

187

Mango-Nectarine Marmalade

مربة أبمأنكؤ وُخؤخ
M'rabah ab Mango oo Choch

This recipe is my mother's recipe. As a child, I often asked her to make it. I especially liked it because she left some larger pieces of fruit in the jam. Now, my family loves it; they use it as a topping over ice cream and sprinkle it with chopped fresh fruit and chopped nuts.

2 large lemons	1 cup honey
4 large mangoes, peeled and chopped	½ teaspoon ground ginger
1 large nectarine, peeled and chopped	¼ teaspoon ground cinnamon
1 cup sugar	¼ teaspoon ground cardamom

Grate the skins from 1 of the lemons and set aside. Make lemon juice from the grated lemon. Peel the remaining lemon, slice it, and remove the seeds.

Combine the mango, nectarine, 1½ cups of water, sugar, honey, lemon skin, lemon juice, lemon slices, ginger, cinnamon, and cardamom in a pot. Bring to a boil over high heat. Reduce heat to low and simmer for 15 minutes. Remove from heat, chill, and transfer to the sanitized jars (see page 183). Seal the jars and refrigerate. Mango-Nectarine Marmalade keeps for 2 months.

Index of Recipes

Mama Nazima's Jewish-Iraqi Cuisine

Index of Stories

References

Berg, N. E. *Exile from Exile—Israeli Writers from Iraq* (Albany, NY: State University of New York Press, 1996)

Eban, A. *My People—Abba Eban's History of the Jews* adapted by D. Bamberger (New York: Behrman House Press, 1978)

Gordon, A. *How to Strengthen the Immune System* (Torrance, CA: Homestead Schools Inc., 1998)

Kazzaz, D., *Mother of the Pound* (Brooklyn, NY: Sepher-Hermon Press, 1999)

Lewis, B. *The Jews of Islam* (Princeton, NJ: Princeton Univerity Press, 1984)

Roth, C. *History of the Jews* (New York: Shocken Books, 1965)

www.ingramcontent.com/pod-product-compliance
Lightning Source LLC
Jackson TN
JSHW011401130125
77033JS00023B/781